T0206992

Unreal for Mobile and Standalone VR

Create Professional VR Apps Without Coding

Cornel Hillmann

Apress®

Unreal for Mobile and Standalone VR: Create Professional VR Apps
Without Coding

Cornel Hillmann
Singapore, Singapore

ISBN-13 (pbk): 978-1-4842-4359-6   ISBN-13 (electronic): 978-1-4842-4360-2
https://doi.org/10.1007/978-1-4842-4360-2

Managing Director, Apress Media LLC: Welmoed Spahr
Acquisitions Editor: Natalie Pao
Development Editor: James Markham
Coordinating Editor: Jessica Vakili

Cover designed by eStudioCalamar

Cover image designed by Freepik (www.freepik.com)

Distributed to the book trade worldwide by Springer Science+Business Media New York, 233 Spring Street, 6th Floor, New York, NY 10013. Phone 1-800-SPRINGER, fax (201) 348-4505, e-mail orders-ny@springer-sbm.com, or visit www.springeronline.com. Apress Media, LLC is a California LLC and the sole member (owner) is Springer Science + Business Media Finance Inc (SSBM Finance Inc). SSBM Finance Inc is a Delaware corporation.

For information on translations, please e-mail rights@apress.com, or visit http://www.apress.com/rights-permissions.

Apress titles may be purchased in bulk for academic, corporate, or promotional use. eBook versions and licenses are also available for most titles. For more information, reference our Print and eBook Bulk Sales web page at http://www.apress.com/bulk-sales.

Any source code or other supplementary material referenced by the author in this book is available to readers on GitHub via the book's product page, located at www.apress.com/978-1-4842-4359-6. For more detailed information, please visit http://www.apress.com/source-code.

Printed on acid-free paper

For Audrey and Lenoir

Table of Contents

TABLE OF CONTENTS

About the Author

Cornel Hillmann is a Computer Graphics (CG) artist, virtual reality developer, and entrepreneur, and runs `studio.cgartist.com`, where he provides design, visualization, and VR services for his B2B clients.

Cornel started his career as an art director in Los Angeles after receiving his diploma in computer graphics. He founded CNT Media GmbH a media production company in Hamburg, Germany, and Emerging Entertainment Pte. Ltd., based in Singapore. Over the years, he has produced interactive media applications, visualizations, and animations for corporate clients and design partners and has helped media companies as a consultant to optimize their production pipeline. Cornel has produced a line of training video DVDs on the subject of 3D modeling, animation, and visual effects. He has also lectured on the subjects of character animation, design, and virtual reality. He has often contributed to development conferences and interactive media events as a panel member and speaker. Cornel became involved in VR with the first Oculus developer kit in 2013. While using Unity 3D, he moved over to Unreal in 2014. Since then, he has integrated Unreal into his workflow using it as a production environment developing interactive visualizations for his product design and media clients, while secretly working on his own VR mystery game during his spare time.

About the Technical Reviewer

Wojciech Jakóbczyk is a senior software professional with experience in various industries. For the last few years, he has been engaged in virtual reality development—mostly technologies for content creation. He has experience working with Unreal Engine 4 on VR platforms ranging from mobile and standalone to high-end desktop headsets. Currently, he is working as a CTO at Superbright (`www.superbright.org`), a VR content studio developing games and other interactive VR experiences.

Acknowledgement

First, I would like to thank my wife, Audrey, for her support and patience as a consultant, concept proofreader, and test audience.

My thanks go out to fellow VR developer Hampus Soderstrom, the ingenious mind behind the classic cult game *Toribash: Violence Perfected*. He got me started in VR, and thanks to him, I was able to get the first Oculus dev-kit 1 in the early VR days, when it was very difficult to get a hold of one. Hampus is the creator of the crazy-wild VR titles *Boxplosion*, *Actionpaint VR*, and *Dimensional Intersection* on Steam VR (do yourself a favor and check them out, as they are a lot of fun).

I would also like to thank Carl-Emil Kjellstrand for hooking me up with the northern European developer scene through his invitation to speak at the Øredev conference, which has resulted in a lot of new professional friendships, partnerships, and inspirations for future endeavors.

I would also like to thank Joanna Adams, the creative director and author behind *The Future is Wild* TV series. The teamwork to produce the first *The Future is Wild* VR showcase at the MIPCOM conference in Cannes, France, was rewarded with a lot of enthusiasm, positive feedback, and new opportunities.

My thanks to my visualization and design clients and partners, whose projects have supported me over the years.

I should also thank my VR course students, who helped me discover new angles in prototyping during class and made it fun to explore new VR concepts. Last but not least, I'd like to thank my fellow VR developers and colleagues in Singapore, including the Asia VR Association, for the community support, enthusiasm, and fun events, and prototype and technology demos that help make this industry as exciting as it is.

Preface

The Unreal engine has had, for the longest time, the reputation to be used only in major game productions with large teams and budgets in the seven- to eight-digit range and therefore not being very accessible to smaller studios or individual designers to produce interactive visualizations.

This perception is now being challenged as it has become an accessible and reliable tool for real-time visualization in the architecture and product design industry. Real-time graphics are replacing render farm–based production pipelines for animation productions, and visual scripting is making software development accessible to creatives.

Due to the high-end history of the Unreal engine, most literature have been focused on C++ coders and not so much on designers, artists and creators coming from the visual arts field, even though Unreal brings a perfect toolset and production environment for the creative mind.

This book caters to visual artists coming from a traditional 3D background. It only requires an understanding of Unreal engine basics, which can quickly and easily be learned from the Unreal online educational resources. Basic understanding of the interface and being familiar with the most important components for an Unreal project are required as prerequisites. It is recommended to be familiar with the different types of variables and Blueprint classes.

In the hands-on section of the book, we will cover the basic setup for locomotion, teleportation, and motion controller interaction and complete two project-based tutorials. The first is a fully interactive VR product presentation using the widget interaction components and the second is a project focused on puzzle mechanics and AI characters in Chapter 7.

The instructions cover not only Unreal but also the full roundtrip using Blender, Substance Designer, Substance Painter, and other typical production tools.

All of the examples and tutorials have been chosen to work within a book format. Blueprints can easily grow in complexity; for that reason, we will try to keep the focus on the most essential parts. Feel free to add your own refinements to extend the basic setup to a customized and extended final result. The format of this book was inspired by a development journal, where the detailed description of a Blueprint execution is followed by a screenshot image. This way, it can easily be used as a reference, when coming back to it later. The chapters on optimization, pipelines, concepting, references, ecosystems, and outlook are provided to give a complete roundup of all the factors that play into a VR production and hopefully they provide a glimpse into the exciting VR future that is ahead of us.

This book is intended as an introduction, guide, and hands-on tutorial to virtual reality (VR) production using the Unreal engine. It is intended for designers, artists and multimedia producers interested in expanding their toolset. The new generation of mobile and standalone VR headsets is finally reaching the mainstream of consumers. For content producers, devices such as the Oculus Go offer a solid platform for immersive content and the Unreal engine a proven workhorse for mobile and standalone VR development.

As VR headsets have become more affordable, and easier to use along with increased display quality, adoption rates have accelerated. Today, it is not uncommon to see VR headsets—not only at convention booths, but also at local car dealerships, supermarkets, and shopping malls—being used to introduce consumers to new products, services, and promotions, as well as to provide entertainment at home.

This book aims to give a foundation to approaching and executing a VR production with two different examples. The first tutorial project focuses on visualization and techniques to tweak the rendering quality by looking at light mapping techniques, among others. The second tutorial project gives a deeper look into Blueprint interactions to understand how a light puzzle-style experience is laid out. This example is not limited to use for games, but can also be applied to the gamification of other content.

A Brief History of Unreal and VR

VR has come a long way, from its humble beginnings in the early '90s, when it was first commercially introduced, to the years behind closed doors in high-end research facilities, up until its most recent incarnation, when the startup Oculus launched its Kickstarter campaign for the Oculus Rift in 2012, and finally its purchase by Facebook for two billion dollars.

From Tethered to Mobile and Standalone VR

When the new generation of VR head mounted devices (HMDs), spearheaded by the Oculus Rift and the HTC Vive was introduced in 2016, the industry was at first in for a bumpy ride as unrealistic market expectations, hype and high ownership costs prevented a commercial breakthrough and kept the user base limited to a niche of enthusiasts and special interest users.

The latest wave of mobile and standalone VR HMDs based on the Android operating system is finally breaking out of this niche and gaining traction with low cost, ease of use and high quality offerings.

While devices such as the Vive Focus and the Lenovo Mirage Solo are using six degrees of freedom (6DOF) tracking on players' orientation through the headset similar to high-end PC-based VR setups, all of these devices, including the Oculus Go, include one common feature—a three degrees of freedom (3DOF) motion controller that only tracks the user's hand rotational movements.

There has been a heated discussion among users and developers as to what extent is 6DOF more critically important than 3DOF for a solid VR experience. Whichever camp you are in, when it comes to 6DOF, it is only a matter of time until mobile and standalone VR is on par with PC-based tethered headsets. The same is true for visual fidelity, as we are approaching cloud-based VR, enabled through high-performance 5G networks in the not-too-distant future.

Mobile and standalone VR is the future, and the Oculus Go is the first consumer-friendly generation of this device category, as it presents itself with the best value and price-performance ratio. For this reason, this book is focused on development for the Oculus Go. The principles and techniques will fundamentally be the same for subsequent generations of this device category, when 6DOF and other technical enhancements will find its way to the next generation of mobile and standalone VR HMDs.

The New Era of Digital Content Creation with Visual Scripting

To develop for VR we have two major contenders: The Unreal Engine by Epic Games and Unity 3D, both excellent choices in their own ways. The Unreal engine has the advantage of the fully integrated visual scripting system called Blueprints, a successor to the previous, much more limited visual scripting system called Kismet in Unreal 3. Even though there are third-party visual scripting plugins for Unity 3D, nothing comes close to the deep integration into the engine as we have in Unreal 4 with Blueprints. The power of visual scripting is that it opens the doors to non-coders. Today it is possible to do complete productions without writing a single line of code, something unthinkable just a decade ago. Blueprints can be as complex as you want them to be; the possibilities are limitless. By creating game logic with a nodes-based interface, digital artists, multimedia producers or level designers have access to everything needed to complete and deploy a final application.

Some people even learn coding by understanding how Blueprints works. By diving deep into the world of Blueprints, programming principles and terminology becomes clearer and more illustrated. The native programming language of Unreal is C++, with full source code access for developers. Big productions will of course base their development to a good extent on C++, especially in challenging areas such as complex multiplayer projects. But for smaller teams, or even the typical one-man show, Blueprints is all you need. Internally, Blueprints run in what is called a virtual machine, an intermediate abstraction, instead of on a compiled machine code. In case there are concerns for performance, it is even possible to cook Blueprints into C++ code, so even that concern is taken care of.

Nevertheless, for performance optimization, it is also important to understand the typical coding bottlenecks, such as unnecessary ticks. Very often, when a complex Blueprint system is designed in Unreal, it does not hurt to have a programmer look at it, to see if the structure could use improvements.

Real-Time Graphics Beyond Games: A Paradigm Shift

Next to the incredible Blueprint powerhouse that Unreal provides, the quality of the real-time graphics sets it apart.

High-end real-time visualization using the Unreal engine has in recent years disrupted the design- and architectural visualization-industry. What we are witnessing is a paradigm shift from pre-rendered imaging, using costly pipelines and render farms to a much more efficient physically based rendering (PBR) based real-time workflow using game engines powered by the latest high-end graphics cards.

Even though the excellent Unity 3D engine is catching up, Unreal reigns supreme in visual quality. In fact, the breakthroughs in architectural visualizations using Unreal have made their way into film production and TV commercials. Epic games, the company behind Unreal, is working hard to stay on the bleeding edge of entertainment technology by showcasing real-time live performance capture systems that offer an alternative to traditional pipelines in the movie industry.

Before 2014, Unreal was not very accessible to the average independent studio. Since its beginnings in 1998, the Unreal toolset was limited to AAA developers who could afford the minimum six-digit licensing fees. It was a small exclusive club of high-end studios who were given access to the technology behind games such as *Bioshock*, *Gears of War*, and of course, *Unreal Tournament* itself. What triggered the revolution for Unreal to open up was the success of Unity 3D.

Unity 3D had its early beginnings on Mac OS in 2005. With the rise of indies and mobile gaming, it quickly became a huge success and started to conquer other platforms. The reasons were obvious: Before Unity 3D, game development was a complicated and extremely technical process. Indie developers, who did not have access to the tools of AAA studios as Unreal, had to integrate various middleware solutions with their own libraries. When Unity 3D came along, it had all those components integrated and unified, thus the name Unity. Plus, the base version was free. Unity 3D took the industry by storm—a storm that turned into a hurricane that was starting to eat into the territory of Unreal.

In 2015, having changed their licensing model, Unreal the engine became free to download and use by anyone, with the only condition that the user pays five percent royalties on the gross income of any title that is produced with Unreal. It was a fair deal that helped the company to succeed in the years to come. Today the company is as strong as ever, with huge cross-platform hits such as *Fortnite* under its belt. While Unity 3D is dominating the industry with the number of developers, it is Unreal that is generating the most revenue for its developers.

Unreal today is a powerhouse that is expanding from games into film, live performances, and the visualization industry. And, of course, it has been one of the driving forces behind the new generation of VR.

Industry Visionaries Pushing the Boundaries

The man behind Unreal, CEO and developer legend Tim Sweeney, is one of the most respected visionaries of the industry. He represents the company culture at Epic games, which keeps pushing the boundaries of interactive entertainment.

The same can be said for the man behind the Oculus Go: John Carmack, CTO of Oculus, a legend in his own right and regarded as the father of modern gaming. Carmack basically invented 3D gaming in the early '90s with innovation breakthroughs such as Wolfenstein 3D and Doom. As a CTO at Oculus, he was one of the forces behind the new generation of VR. His focus has been mobile and standalone VR. The Oculus Go is a result of his efforts in micro-optimizing the hardware and software to extreme levels.

Recognizing the exceptional genius and leadership by industry legends such as Tim Sweeney for Unreal and John Carmack for the Oculus Go is a good way of feeling confident about the future of mobile and standalone VR. The technology that we use today is the result of a culture of innovation that goes back two to three decades, of trial and error, of optimizations and breakthrough ideas.

Taking Immersive Media to the Next Level

The innovation in gaming technology today is benefiting other areas, such as interactive media production, which was decades ago dominated by tools such as Macromedia/Adobe Director or Virtools by Dassault Systèmes. The Unreal engine is flexible enough to power interactive product presentations, learning applications and enterprise solutions.

Serious games, used for business simulation, data visualization, and exploratory learning, are very often benefiting when done in VR, especially when scale plays an important role or immersion enhances the simulated experience. In most cases, mobile and standalone VR is the way to go, as it is the most user-friendly, hassle-free, and cost-effective way to bring the experience to the user or client.

It is an exciting time to develop for mobile and standalone VR using the Unreal engine. As the industry is maturing and a lot of industries are opening up to immersive simulations, there are a lot of opportunities for developers to be innovative and disruptive. Tourism, health care, education, enterprise, and entertainment are just some of the areas that are at the beginning of a new era in which VR adds value through immersion and increased comprehension of complex visual information.

CHAPTER 1

The VR Ecosystem and What to Expect in the Years to Come

This chapter is a snapshot of the wider virtual reality (VR) industry at the time of the writing of this book. VR innovation is constantly evolving, partly due to the fact that the latest wave of the consumer VR market is still in its early stages; in many aspects, not unlike the early smartphone market, when a large variety of technologies, formats, form factors, and user experience (UX) concepts were competing for consumer attention. Besides the almost daily news on breakthrough research in areas like resolution, eye tracking, and usability, there are stable long-term trends that have proven to be reliable pointers for the roadmap ahead of us. We will look at these established long-term VR trends and evaluate what is relevant in the mobile and standalone VR space.

In later chapters, we look at more specific context, starting with conceptual thoughts in Chapter 3 to a more focused trend forecast for mobile and standalone VR in Chapter 9.

© Cornel Hillmann 2019
C. Hillmann, *Unreal for Mobile and Standalone VR*,
https://doi.org/10.1007/978-1-4842-4360-2_1

The VR Landscape

The VR industry is evolving and becoming increasingly more diverse. The latest wave of VR evolution started in 2012, with the enormously successful Kickstarter campaign by the first incarnation of Oculus. Before 2012, VR mostly lived in research facilities and highly specialized industrial applications; for example, long-term virtual reality training software developers such as EON Reality.

The initial spark by Oculus ignited renewed consumer interest in the technology, after it had almost been forgotten since the early VR hype in the 1990s, when it peaked and then quickly folded after devices like Nintendo's Virtual Boy console in 1995 couldn't convince consumers. Although the technology was not ready in the 1990s, the current advance in 3D graphics processing finally made the latest VR generation consumer-friendly, both in terms of quality and cost. A new wave of VR development spread around the globe, and with new technology breakthroughs came VR developers, agencies, startups, organizations, events, expos, pop-up theatres and a wide spread of VR meetups, where enthusiasts shared their prototypes and insights.

The other big impact came out of Taiwan. The Vive brand, launched by smartphone producer HTC, gained traction with enthusiasts and developers due to their uncompromised commitment to high-end quality in VR using the SteamVR Lighthouse tracking technology developed by Valve Corporation.

The third big player in the VR space is Google, since the first wide distribution of the Google Cardboard, followed by the Daydream mobile headset up to the latest iteration of 6DOF headsets licensed to Lenovo. Microsoft, on the other hand, can be credited as having brought inside-out tracking to the consumer market and the wide variety of headsets in the Microsoft Windows mixed-reality space is slowly expanding its user base.

Next to the big players, there are numerous one-offs—specialized and experimental hardware. Some projects, such as the ambitious OSVR (open source VR) platform and its supported devices, have almost completely disappeared. WebVR is rebounding as a hardware agnostic platform with a lot of developers getting behind it, and the amount of specialized experimental hardware for haptic and locomotion accessories is constantly expanding.

PC-based Tethered VR and Consoles

In terms of basic hardware platforms, it makes sense to differentiate by the type of tracking used. PC-based tethered systems such as the Oculus Rift and the HTC Vive use outside-in motion tracking based on optical tracking toward the headset from a stationary position, such as the SteamVR Lighthouse system. Windows MR headsets use inside-out tracking. A number of specialized headsets promise to support both tracking solutions, such as the Chinese Pimax 8K (which is actually 2 × 4K).

Almost all PC-based VR HMDs have access to the titles on the Valve Corporation's distribution platform, Steam, which is also the dominant platform for digital games distribution in general. For this reason, Steam market data provides a good base for analyzing the health and diversity of the VR ecosystem. Looking at the statistics, we can clearly see that the Oculus Rift is overtaking the HTC Vive in market penetration. The data also shows that Windows MR HMDs are slowly gaining ground, as mentioned early.

PC-based tethered VR is slowly growing at a steady pace, but it remains a niche for enthusiasts. Nevertheless, industry veterans very often point out that this is exactly what PC gaming looked like in the days before it became mainstream. A number of factors make it plausible that PC-based VR will get a push in the near future. Valve Corporation, operators of the Steam platform, and producers of legendary titles such as *Half-Life*, *Portal*, *Team Fortress 2*, and *Dota 2*, confirmed their commitment to PC-based VR by announcing three big VR titles in production that will most likely take advantage of the new controller currently being tested by the company's development team.

It is safe to say that at least for the hardcore gaming crowd, PC-based tethered VR will get a big boost when Valve rolls out their new lineup of VR titles, should they be successful. In the meantime, Oculus and HTC are offering new incentives to developers with development grants and accelerator programs. The Oculus store is expanding its lineup of impressive VR titles, and HTC is pushing Viveport as an alternative, especially in Asian regions where Valve and Oculus have little market access.

Besides PC-based VR, Sony's PlayStation VR (PSVR) is (so far) the only gaming console with a VR HMD extension. The advantage of PSVR is a well-designed headset that is comfortable to wear and has a screen with a good pixel fill. This means that although the resolution is lower than the average PC-based VR HMD, the dreaded "screen door" effect (the space between each pixel) is hardly visible due to the PSVR's penile subpixel arrangement, which, therefore, gives a much smoother image impression, even though the lower resolution occasionally generates digital artifacts. Besides the fact that the PSVR motion controller lacks accuracy, overall it is a complete package with a good selection of AAA titles to choose from.

A special highlight of PSVR is the support of the PlayStation VR Aim controller on a number of titles, first introduced with the game *Farpoint*. This controller integrates seamlessly as a fully tracked VR rifle and is one of the most highly rated VR accessories available.

Sony's PlayStation VR is a success story, but is also limited by its closed ecosystem. For this reason, it is very unlikely that a developer would choose PSVR as an enterprise VR platform. For consumers, it is an interesting entry point into VR for a moderate price, based on hardware that is already a part of many living rooms.

VR Arcades

The arcade business is a special sector in which tethered VR HMDs are being used. VR arcades have proven to be a solid business and not to be a fad, as feared initially. Very often, VR arcades provide the highest-end VR tech available and charge by the hour or the minute. Typical setups include full body and gun tracking with haptic feedback via gun recoil, a backpack PC, and a custom multiplayer experience. The HTC Vive and the Vive Pro dominate the arcade market, but other players, such as StarVR, with higher resolution and higher field of view HMDs, are aiming to shoot for a premium segment in the arcade world.

VR arcades are part of the out-of-home segment in the VR market. Early success stories have shown that they are here to stay and that they provide a testing ground for bleeding-edge VR technology that may later find its way into lower-cost VR hardware.

Next-generation VR hardware does not only involve improved display technology and extended tracking through full-body tracing systems such as OptiTrack, but also provide extended options for physical accessories beyond the VR riffle. HTC's Vive Tracker is designed to take in this task. The palm-size device ties seamlessly into SteamVR for 6DOF tracking, a micro USB port allows custom functions to be picked up by the attached device, and the data is transmitted directly to a USB dongle on the supporting PC.

Arcade developers have used this device to experiment with custom controllers, such as tennis rackets, baseball bats, gym gear, and a variety of guns. Custom controllers, when mirrored accurately in the VR experience, give an added immersive value that is partially due to the haptic interaction with the controller. It can be expected that external VR gear will find its way to future generations of mobile and standalone VR once the technical hurdles of external tracking for Android devices have been solved in a way that makes performance and cost factors more consumer friendly.

The overwhelming success of Nintendo's Wii accessory ecosystem, including rackets, steering wheels, golf bats, and musical instruments, have been a powerful showcase for how much consumers appreciate haptical controller input for electronic entertainment.

High Visual Quality: A Crucial Factor for Success

One of the most crucial factors in VR gaining a wider audience is the visual quality of the picture generated by the headsets. Consumers have become accustomed to high-resolution TVs and mobile screens. While hardcore gamers may prioritize game mechanics over pixel resolution, a casual VR consumer with a focus on having a short break in VR, or watching an immersive video, has a much higher expectation of the display quality. Enterprise, educational, and healthcare application use cases for VR are also very sensitive to display quality, because display text often plays an important role in on-screen instructions and contextual information layers, which make it hard to read on a display lacking pixel density.

Increased Field of View: Another Crucial Factor for Success

A second crucial factor is the field of view (FoV), which determines how much the user is immersed and the often-quoted sensation of "presence" in the VR world is accomplished. It should be noted that the success of the first developer kit (DK1) of the Oculus Rift was largely due to the much higher FoV than previous headset concepts. VR prototypes have been on show at gaming conventions prior to the Oculus DK1; they provided the same basic setup—3DOF stereoscopic view of the game environment, but the limited FoV made the experience similar to looking through a binocular.

The Oculus DK1 achieved a FoV of more than 110 degrees diagonally, which proved to be a game changer for immersiveness at that time. Human perception is highly sensitive to FoV, where every single degree counts, and the cutoff point or VR presence is around 90 to 100 degrees, depending on the individual. It is safe to say that a FoV over 100 degrees is crucial to an immersive VR experience. The human binocular FoV is around 200 to 220 degrees. While specialized HMDs such as Pimax and StarVR come closer to that number, the majority of PC-tethered VR HMDs have a long way to go.

One of the hurdles that the industry has to overcome is the high GPU processing power required to run larger display panels that can cover a larger FoV. As the total ownership cost of tethered VR setups is already very high due to the high minimum specs, the additional power required to support the higher resolution for better pixel density and wider FoV will make these systems even more costly, and therefore, will exclude the majority of consumers. Nevertheless, there are innovative approaches on the way to improve image quality in VR. Hopes are high for foveated rendering, using eye tracking, which only renders the highest pixel density in the viewers' focus area, and thus requires less GPU horsepower in running high-resolution display panels.

The little sister of eye-tracked foveated rendering is *lens-based foveated rendering*, often referred to as *fixed foveated rendering* or FFR. Fixed foveated rendering divides the screen in different zones and prioritizes the center areas of the viewing area, so that the heavy processing load and pixel density are not wasted on areas that are less seen by the user. This approach was used on the Oculus Go, and it was recently added to the Rift as well. It is very likely that foveated rendering using eye tracking will find its way from research labs to the consumer in the near future.

It is pretty safe to assume that we'll see eye tracking and higher pixel density displays with a wider field of view in the following generation of PC-based VR headsets, along with larger area full-body tracking and ecosystem of trackable accessories and integrated wireless transmitters. Lighter VR headsets that are easier to strap on and less bulky-looking, will help consumer adoption. There have been a number of concepts by fashion designers to integrate VR HMDs into futuristic outfit designs. When these take a center stage at public events, and VR becomes a fashion statement, it most likely means VR is moving into the mainstream.

Mobile and Standalone VR

While PC-based VR may have a great future in leading the new frontier in high-end VR, it is mobile and standalone VR that is the most exciting area for businesses and developers looking for growth, flexibility, and mass market appeal. The success story of mobile and standalone VR began when media companies and marketers used the super low-end Google Cardboard viewer for high-volume campaigns.

The famous The Displaced campaign by *The New York Times*, for example, used VR as the often-quoted "empathy machine" by immersing the viewer into the grim reality of Syrian refugees by viewing an immersive VR video. The simple viewing app was available for download from the iPhone App Store, as well as the Google Play Store for Android devices. The foldable cardboard viewer was easy to include in mailings, magazine inserts, and handouts. By the year 2017, Google had shipped 10 million of these simple VR viewers, and for a lot of consumers, this was their first introduction to the basic concept of VR, even though low-resolution, limited FoV and the lack of a controller led to a very limited VR experience only remotely related to a proper VR setup.

While the Google VR boxes spread in various variations, including numerous spin-offs out of China, VR advocates worried that this kind of bare-bones low-end VR could actually damage the reputation of the VR industry and possibly turn consumers away.

Google has since evolved the Cardboard concept into Google VR, which now includes its own high-quality Daydream platform, which is similar to the Gear VR, and a standalone VR version with 6DOF headset tracking. The Lenovo Mirage Solo was the first HMD to be based on technology called WorldSense.

Samsung Gear VR, Oculus Go, and Beyond

The biggest success story of first-generation mobile VR is the Samsung Gear VR, powered by Oculus software. It provides a solid mobile VR experience in terms of resolution and FoV, using the latest-generation Samsung smartphones. According to market data, in 2017, the Gear VR passed ten million units sold. A lot of these units were bundled with sales promotions or giveaways. Nevertheless, the Gear VR app store, powered by Oculus, has grown to more than 1,000 apps. It was a smart move by Oculus to tag along with Samsung's huge mobile market reach, and then build the first low-cost standalone, the Oculus Go, on that foundation.

The Oculus Go is a step up from the Gear VR in all areas: an LCD display with better pixel density, an improved lens, and FoV and integrated spatial audio speakers. The design allows the user to jump straight into VR without any of the friction usually associated with VR HMDs. The controller has a better haptic feel, and the overheating issue that troubled earlier Gear VRs has been tackled with a well-designed internal heat sink.

At its competitive price point, the Go is the first true VR consumer product. Future generations of this device category will most likely add 6DOF, access to the VR cloud through 5G, plus possibly VR accessories. The Go was launched in China under the Xiaomi brand, which is the actual manufacturer of the headset. Next to the Pico Neo HMD it is another player in the vibrant Chinese VR market.

The main competitors to the Oculus Go are the Vive Focus, a high-quality standalone 6DOF HMD, and the Lenovo Mirage Solo, with similar specs, but at more than double the price of the Oculus Go.

Use Cases

Besides being more accessible, easier to use, and more affordable, mobile and standalone VR HMDs have a number of important advantages over tethered PC-based systems. For businesses, it is an easy solution to present immersive product presentations and previsualizations to an experience area at a convention booth or to take it to a client. Very often, previsualizations (as in the architectural or product design sector) are already designed for real-time interactivity, with assets optimized and ready for VR. In such cases, adding a VR experience to a previsualization job requires only a limited extra amount of additional work.

For this reason, Epic released an extra subscription-based version of the Unreal Engine targeted at the design industry, with the benefit of optimized import capabilities for CAD formats using the Unreal Datasmith conversion pipeline that supports a large number of content creation tools and formats, plus templates and a large material asset library.

Bringing design content—including data from the architectural, engineering, and construction (AEC) industries—into the engine is the first step in deploying the content to mobile VR HMDs, once it has been optimized and properly staged for VR.

In the B2B sector, VR is already an established way of presenting concepts and visualization. Mobile and standalone VR HMDs such as the Samsung Gear and the Oculus Go bring the flexibility and mobility that design professionals need.

For consumers, the benefits of mobile and standalone VR is even more obvious. The headset provides an easy break when traveling on long flights and in waiting areas. It is a good way to escape on the living room couch or an alternative way to talk to friends by meeting up in one of the social VR spaces. Social VR is becoming one of the most important driving forces for consumer VR. While social apps such as AltspaceVR have been around since the early VR days, it is the combination of social spaces, such as Oculus rooms with launch pads to multiplayer experiences that add value to the social experience.

Meeting as avatars adds a unique feeling of presence that cannot be compared to a video chat. Launching from a social VR space into a multiplayer experience with a friend in a remote location is perceived as an attractive feature to consumers. Social aspects also play a role for VR business apps. For example, Oculus rooms can be used for small presentations with up to four people by using the media area in these rooms to host slideshows on a large wall-mounted screen. The source of slides is the paired phone's image library.

An additional use of mobile and standalone VR that has a social aspect to it is corporate groups training, not only for skills learning, but also for motivational and behavioral purposes. A user wearing a VR headset can be brought into a special situation, and his communication with his team members can be monitored and analyzed. For small applications that have to be customized for each event, WebVR is a great tool. Gear VR and the Oculus Go have an integrated web browser. The latest generation of WebVR tools, such as A-Frame, makes app development fast and accessible to multimedia designers because it uses JavaScript.

For small events for which custom apps need to be tweaked at the last minute, and according to the audience specifications, these tools are a great solution. WebVR has come a long way and can deliver convincing and rich VR experiences, especially for the educational and training field.

The Reality Race: VR vs. AR

Looking at the VR ecosystem, there has been a noticeable trend that VR designers–especially in the UX field—are transitioning to using the term *XR* (extended reality) rather than *VR*. This makes total sense because XR is the umbrella term for VR, AR (augmented reality), and MR (mixed reality), especially as interest in AR is surging. ARKit from Apple, and ARCore from Google, are both supported by the Unreal Engine, which means that user efficiency in Unreal is also applicable when exploring AR solutions for a project that was initially only meant to be in VR.

Growth in the VR industry has been moderate in comparison to the high expectations that the initial media hype triggered. This is one of the reasons why some developers have turned their attention from VR to AR. AR is hailed to a much larger market with better use cases and more potential to innovate productivity apps.

This trend has created unrealistic expectations for consumers in what AR can deliver in the near future. From the way it is portrayed in mass media and marketing, consumers expect the coming generation of AR wearables to offer full immersion and object recognition while tracking the environment.

The reality is that even with the latest generation of leading AR HMDs, such as the HoloLens and Magic Leap, these features are way in the future. The current generation of AR headsets has a much more reduced FoV than the current generation of VR headsets, and the tracking technology is limited to planar surfaces, such as floor, wall, ceiling, and slanted areas. Individual objects are only recognized if image markers are embedded. AR is really years away from fully understanding the environment. Once AI machine learning gets to the point that environment objects can be better understood and processed in real time so that meaningful user interaction can add value to the experience, it will be an exciting field for consumer applications. However, it is a work in progress with a long way ahead of it. Even as this area is rapidly evolving, VR is a matured technology that is available to the consumer, while immersive AR wearables still have a long way to go.

One interesting development is that a number of VR headsets have front cameras and allow camera pass-through, which has the potential to bridge the VR and AR worlds. Once quality issues, such as camera latency, have been resolved, new ways to transition between AR and VR will open up. For example, a tabletop AR board game could temporarily be moved into VR space to add environment features, and after a while, seamlessly move back to the AR setting. Seamless AR to VR will be the most consumer-friendly transition into VR. The term *XR* already holds that promise in its name definition.

AR has been established in mobile application via camera overlays, such as in Snapchat filters, and in enterprise learning and productivity solutions, but immersive AR via wearable HMDs are nowhere near as consumer-ready as VR HMDs are. Once Apple makes its market entry with an AR wearable, and Magic Leap and its competitors reveal their final products, VR headsets will enter the next level of evolution and refinement.

The Oculus Go is really the first matured consumer product of the entire XR field, and this device category is expected to maintain its head-start advantage through future iterations.

For this reason, this book focuses on developing for the Oculus Go. The same basic development principles that apply to standalone Android apps for the Go apply to the next-generation 6DOF headset.

For content creators, 3D artists, and multimedia designers, this platform is an incredible opportunity to bring full-scale, real-time interactivity to 3D creation. And, the sophisticated toolset of the Unreal Engine makes it a pleasure to create and optimize content, whether visualizations, games, or other kinds of immersive experiences.

Conclusion

This first chapter looked at the broader VR ecosystem in terms of hardware and technologies used, and evaluated the overall market segmentation. We identified the main players in the VR space and looked at what differentiates them. Looking at tethered-VR, arcade application, and the console-based PSVR, we rounded up the diverse VR markets and their unique qualities. We discussed the factors that are important for consumer adoption, and we compared high-end VR vs. mobile and standalone solutions for various use cases. In addition, we evaluated VR in the context of the wider XR field, including AR and MR, and where these technologies stand in their development stages. In the last segment, we concluded that mobile and standalone VR are currently the forerunners of consumer adoption and will most likely lead the industry into larger mainstream adoption as the technology is refined and becomes widely available at a more attractive price point.

CHAPTER 2

VR Production Tools, Workflow, and Pipeline

In this chapter, we go over the basic concepts of creating content for VR, such as generating prerendered stereoscopic 360 VR images, workflows for VR real-time 3D assets and the typical production steps using popular 3D programs. We will also go through the steps to create a real-time 3D asset using the photogrammetry technique. We will look at the key advantages that the Unreal Engine has to offer for VR production and go over common VR production principles to ensure a smooth user experience.

In the last section, we will explore important techniques for immersive VR productions, such as spatial audio, UI and locomotion considerations. At the end of this chapter, you should have an overview of the production principles and techniques and what areas to pay attention to when designing a VR project.

© Cornel Hillmann 2019
C. Hillmann, *Unreal for Mobile and Standalone VR*,
https://doi.org/10.1007/978-1-4842-4360-2_2

VR Video and Images vs. Real-Time Graphics

Depending on the use case, the budget, and the target platform, VR producers have a number of production options to choose from. Very often, the decision has to be made, whether the VR app will be based on real-time graphics, or whether a solution that uses prerendered images to present a project in VR is more appropriate. The typical examples for prerendered VR experiences are real-estate presentations, interactive museums and galleries, or a product showcase.

Prerendered VR sacrifices interactivity for high-fidelity visuals and is very often the more budget-conscious form of presenting content in a VR headset. The advantage of prerendered CGI images for VR is that the complexity and scene detail can be limitless, as only the preproduction render times for the stereoscopic 360 image have to be considered, when planning the scene.

This form of VR presentation makes a lot of sense for highly detailed interiors, where it would be difficult, considering performance limitations and high labor intensiveness to optimize all object details for real-time environments. The other reason is that real-estate presentations and gallery and museum apps very often focus on presenting open spaces, instead of object interactions, that require individual, interactive 3D objects in the VR world. For image-based environment VR apps, the interaction typically means activating a hotspot to change the viewing position, where on each position a different prerendered 360 image is loaded.

Unreal is equipped with a very useful plugin that renders stereoscopic images of an Unreal level, as shown in Figure 2-1.

Figure 2-1. *The Stereo Panoramic Movie Plugin captures images and image sequences*

The other option is to render the 360 image in a digital content creation (DCC) software such as Maya, 3D Studio Max, Blender, or Cinema 4D. Most render engines, such as Arnold, V-Ray, Redshift, Octane, and Cycles, support stereoscopic 360 render output. Prerendered stereoscopic 360 images can be a decent solution, when ambient audio plus voice-over narration is added and combined with hotspot teleportation. This form of VR presentation is suitable for a quick and budget-oriented production on a tight deadline. Other than that, this method has also been used for alternative ways of storytelling for experimental and immersive graphic novels in VR, as the stereoscopic VR image format is not constrained to CGI images, but also hand-drawn elements, next to actual 360 photos and video clips, that are captured with the appropriate VR camera rigs.

Increasing VR Video Quality

While a typical VR app based on stereoscopic images is more or less a VR slideshow with audio, the use of stereoscopic 360 video in VR apps is less common, due to the large memory requirements that video entails. The alternative is a download or streaming URL embedded in the Unreal media texture. Common examples are the lobby, or launch pad, for a VR short film, teaser, or even a video platform or short film collection. In such cases, the VR app simply provides the environment for a play VR video button.

Stereoscopic 360 video for standalone headsets is currently a work in progress, as performance and resolution barriers need creative workarounds. One innovative approach was introduced by Oculus CTO John Carmack, for the rerelease of the short film *Henry* by the discontinued Oculus Studios company. By slicing up the film in section segments, he was able to accomplish a 5K × 5K playback at 60 frames per seconds on the Oculus Go, a noticeable bump up in quality from standards VR videos.

Another promising approach is the use of VR180 video, which is a good choice if the action area is centered on just one spot, as it would typically be for a concert or an interview. The advantage of VR180 is that the maxed-out video resolution can be used in the front half of the visual sphere where the center of attention is and therefore allows much higher pixel resolution. The use cases are more geared toward events, or stage performances, and less for exploration-oriented experiences such as a real estate, gallery, or museum presentation, which would not work as well in VR180.

Capturing a Scene with Stereoscopic 360 Images in Unreal

Before moving on to real-time graphics, we will explore the steps that are needed to capture a full Unreal scene in stereoscopic 360 images, merge the left and right views in Photoshop and then drop the combined image into the Oculus Photo app on the Oculus Go headset for review. For this example, we will use a free example scene called *SunTemple* that is provided by Epic Games.

Prerequisites to the tutorial sections are to have signed up, downloaded, and installed the latest version of the free-to-use Unreal Engine by Epic Games, and to be familiar with the interface, such as navigating the viewport, loading, and saving files, including basic interface operations that are necessary to navigate around a scene and its components.

Positioning the Capture Camera

Once we start the Epic Games launcher, we will open the Learn tab in the Unreal Engine section and create a new project based on the *SunTemple* showcase. Next, we enable the Stereo Panoramic Movie Capture Plugin under Edit ➤ Plugins ➤ Movie Capture and restart the editor as requested.

After restarting, double-check that the Plugin checkbox is ticked to be enabled. Load the *SunTemple* scene from your library. Hit the console shortcut (you can assign a shortcut for it in the Menu tab under Edit ➤ Editor Preferences ➤ Keyboard Shortcuts). Search for console command, and input a shortcut of your choice (in our case, we have set it to c instead of the default tilde symbol). Press the Play button and navigate the scene with the W, S, A, and D keys.

Once you have found a position that you would like to capture, open the console with C and enter **sp** in the console, which should bring up all the commands associated with the capture plugin (see Figure 2-2). The list is displayed on top of the console input at the bottom of the window.

Figure 2-2. *The SunTemple scene in Unreal with console and capture commands, ready to be executed*

The first step to capture is to assign a capture directory. We have created a folder called frames on the C drive. To assign the frames folder on the C drive as the output directory, type **SP.OutputDir C:\frames** into the console, and hit Enter. After this step we are ready to capture. We are using the command SP.PanoramicScreenshot.

Stereoscopic Image Processing

Depending on scene complexity and hardware, this may take a moment. Once the process is completed, we should end up with a time-stamped folder in our directory that contains two images indicating left- and right-eye position. While there are ways to automate the process of combining the image into one merged, final stereoscopic image, we will do it manually in Photoshop. The reason being that we may need to run it through an image-processing step to optimize contrast and brightness; hence, we might as well do the image merging there.

In Photoshop, we load both images, left and right, and expand the canvas for the left image from 4096×2048 to 4096×4096. Paste the right image below and export the merged JPG image (see Figure 2-3) to the Pictures directory on the Oculus Go, which is connected via USB.

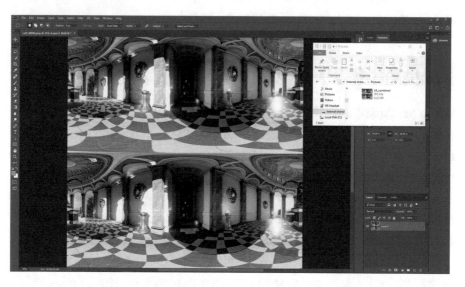

Figure 2-3. *The left and right images have been merged in Photoshop and exported to the Oculus Go*

Reviewing the Stereoscopic 360 Image on the Headset

To review the VR image, put on the Oculus Go headset and navigate to the Oculus Photo app in the library. Inside of the app, choose My Files from the menu on the left, which should display all local images. Once you activate the uploaded image, you are able to explore the 360 stereoscopic panorama of the captured Unreal *SunTemple* scene. This method is a good way to show a client the progress of a visualization project that is at the stage of building environments and graphic assets. By providing a slideshow of a number of high-resolution stereoscopic 360 images, you can give a quick overview of a VR project in development. Captured environments can also be the content type for an image-based VR app.

In Chapter 8, we look at how to use a captured environment as a spherically mapped sky background in Unreal.

Producing 3D Assets for a VR Project

When producing real-time assets, such as 3D models including textures and animations that will be assembled in a VR scene, we have to look at a number of factors, such as target hardware and performance, to make sure that the end result meets the frames-per-second (fps) requirement for VR.

If our VR app is targeting the Oculus Go and the Gear VR, which are binary compatible, we have to look at the hardware range and possibly exclude devices that are under the benchmark target for the visual quality and performance that our project requires. The hardware performance of the Oculus Go is ahead of the Gear VR that uses a Samsung Galaxy S7. For this reason, it makes sense to exclude Samsung devices below that benchmark; namely, the S7 and earlier models.

For our example, we focus solely on the Oculus Go so that we are able to support the Multi-View and OpenGL ES 3.1 features in Unreal (also supported by the S8 and S9 phones). Multi-View reduces the CPU overhead by optimizing the rendering process, and OpenGL ES 3.1 is the latest 3D graphics API supported by Oculus and Unreal.

Hardware and Performance Considerations

When it comes to producing 3D assets for a VR project, we have to keep the hardware limitations in mind and save polygons and textures where we can. For the most part, the asset pipeline is similar as that for 3D mobile games, with the limitation that specific areas work differently in VR.

One such area is the use of normal maps for surface detail, which will only look acceptable in VR if they are in a mid- to far-distance to the viewing camera, due to the fact that normal maps are not stereoscopic and will look flat when viewed up close. Nevertheless, normal maps also play an important role conveying surface complexity through the interaction with lights in a scene, for that reason they are still important in VR.

The other area is physically based render (PBR) materials with dynamic lights, which eat up too much performance when used on too many scene items in full resolution. What it comes down to is balancing scene complexity with texture complexity and detail. Very often, this is a matter of priorities, where the focus is on one hero-item or scene region with full detail and texture complexity while the background information in baked down into a single color map.

Later in the book, we analyze scene complexity with the Unreal optimization toolset to meet the Oculus requirements of 60 fps, 50–100 draw calls per frame, and 50,000–100,000 triangles or vertices per frame.

Pipeline Tools

There are a number of established workflows to produce real-time or game assets. For the examples in this book, we use the following.

- Blender for Polygon and UV editing (`www.blender.org`)

- ZBrush for high-detail sculpting (`www.pixologic.com`)

- Substance Painter and Designer for PBR texture creation and baking (`www.allegorithmic.com`)

- Akeytsu for character animation (`www.nukeygara.com`)

- Toolbag for asset review (`https://marmoset.co/`)

Even though most tasks can be completed with the powerful, free, and open source toolset of Blender, some specialized tools are more efficient for specific tasks. ZBrush is the de facto industry standards for digital sculpting, whereas Substance Painter is the industry's preferred tool for texturing assets. Akeytsu by Nukegara is a great tool for streamlining the otherwise tedious task of rigging and animating characters, and Marmoset Toolbag is an important tool to review assets, especially when working in teams. The combination of these tools allows an efficient digital assets workflow, as shown in Figure 2-4.

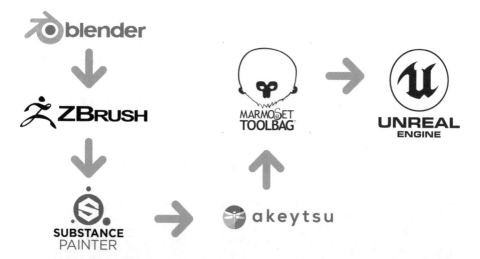

Figure 2-4. *Workflow example from Blender to Unreal, using specialized tools such as Pixologic ZBrush, Allegorithmic Substance Painter, Nukeygara Akeytsu and Marmoset Toolbag*

The asset exchange format FBX is a de facto standard in transferring models, including textures and animations between applications in a production pipeline. Nevertheless, a new emerging file format named glTF 2.0 by the industry consortium Khronos Group, is quickly emerging as a new contender to become the future gold standard for 3D assets. glTF 2.0 is a modern, flexible, and efficient standard with animation and PBR texture support and has strong industry backing.

3D Production Workflow

The typical asset production for a 3D asset starts with a concept or photo. It is recommended to produce the individual asset in a high resolution with a complete PBR texture set, even if the textures will be baked down to a single color texture in lower resolution at a later stage. This way, the maximum flexibility is guaranteed.

The PBR workflow has brought a great degree of standardization to the digital content creation (DCC) ecosystem. Using PBR textures for color, normal, roughness, and metalness allows us to reproduce practically any material surface. It is supported in almost all 3D software.

Let's quickly go over the steps to produce a 3D knife asset to be used in Unreal.

The first step is to produce a clean low-polygon mesh with a good UV map for texture coordinates (as demonstrated in Figure 2-5).

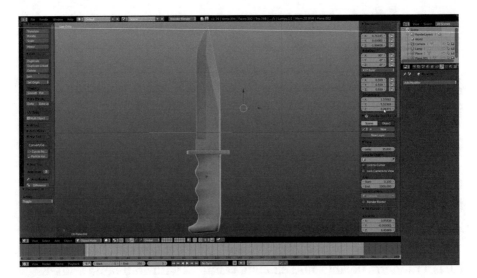

Figure 2-5. *A low polygon knife mesh, modeled in Blender*

Next to a clean mesh, with clearly defined smoothing groups and hard edges, it is most important to have an efficient UV texture map. Before exporting the mesh for texturing, the texture map should be checked for stretching and alignment (see Figure 2-6).

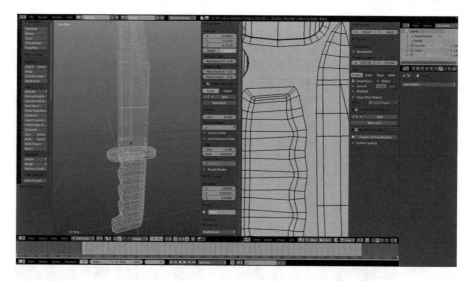

Figure 2-6. *Examining the UV texture coordinates in Blender*

The next step very often involves a high-detail pass in ZBrush. However, in our case, we will skip this step and do some of the fine detail in Substance Painter, after generating a subdivided high-resolution version of the mesh that refines round and sharp areas.

Creating Textures

In Substance Painter, we automatically generate the base maps from the low- and high-polygon mesh and the refine material features of the knife using typical PBR techniques involving layer masks (see Figure 2-7).

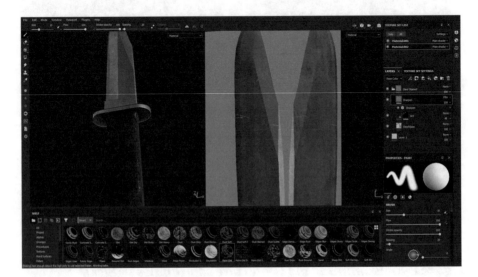

Figure 2-7. *Creating PBR textures in Substance Painter*

Substance Painter has a very useful preset for exporting texture sets to Unreal. The settings of this preset export a color map, a normal map and a combined channel packed map for ambient occlusion, roughness, and metalness; dividing the three channels of an RGB texture into individual outputs for each grayscale texture. The roughness channel uses the green channel, the metallic channel uses the blue channel, and the ambient occlusion channel uses the red channel.

One important step to watch out for is to make sure the occlusion, roughness, and metalness channels are set to linear color instead of sRGB in Unreal or any other rendering application, such as Marmoset Toolbag. The color channel uses sRGB, and the normal channel is usually automatically set to read the normal input.

Previewing Textures

To verify the exported textures from Substance Painter, we will now use Marmoset Toolbag, which is a versatile tool to preview and render 3D assets. We could preview our assets directly in Unreal, but Toolbag allows you to quickly assess a texture set with various different environment lights, making it convenient to detect if a texture or 3D asset has any flaws. In Toolbag, we can quickly get an overview over the PBR texture set (see Figure 2-8) by using the viewer app that comes with the package.

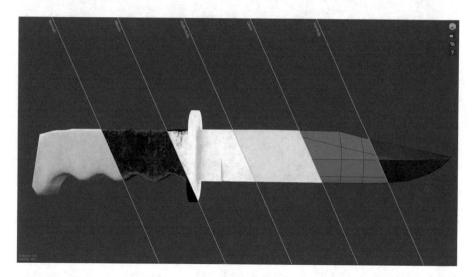

Figure 2-8. *The layer view in the Marmoset view gives a texture-set overview*

Reviewing Models and Textures in Unreal

Importing the verified asset package of low polygon mesh and PBR texture-set into Unreal requires us to set up the materials as defined by the Substance Painter output, as shown in Figure 2-9. Open the imported material, delete the default color texture map, and import the textures by dragging and dropping into the Material editor.

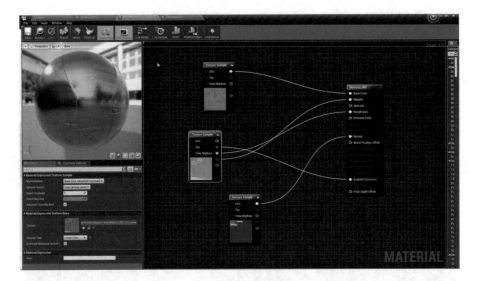

Figure 2-9. *The imported three textures maps connected to one of two materials in the Material editor for the low polygon knife mesh*

After quickly setting up both materials and a quick light rebuild, from the Build menu, we are now ready to review the finished asset in Unreal (see Figure 2-10).

Figure 2-10. *The finished knife in Unreal*

The New Era of Photogrammetry and Volumetric Video

An alternative method for creating assets to be used in Unreal for VR projects is the photogrammetry technique. Photogrammetry has grown in popularity in recent years and enjoys an active community of professionals and enthusiasts that share their creations on platforms such as sketchfab.com.

Photogrammetry software such as Agisoft PhotoScan allows developers to create 3D models from a series of photographs, which at first creates a point cloud and in subsequence steps the geometry and color texture, to reproduce the item in 3D. Photogrammetry objects have the advantage of looking highly realistic, but lack the precision and efficiency of traditionally produced 3D assets. For specific situations, such as projects that involve cultural preservation, history, art, and archeology, photogrammetry is the best solution to re-create lifelike environments and objects that require a high degree of realism. The software algorithms to analyze images have improved considerably in recent years and a lot of innovation is expected in this field.

Volumetric video is a related field on the cutting edge of VR technology that is currently going through bursts of rapid innovation. In a way, volumetric video is photogrammetry with moving images, capturing not only image textures, but also depth information in moving images, which can then be used to generate geometry on the fly. As the technology matures, we can expect new cameras to come out of research labs to make it easier and more affordable to integrate these tools into a VR production. It is one of the most exciting areas of VR and will certainly transform the industry in the coming years.

The Photogrammetry Workflow

In the following steps, we look at how to bring an Asian Garuda statue into the Unreal Engine using Agisoft PhotoScan and a Canon 5D camera. The first step requires us to take enough photos so that the object is covered from all angles; in this case, it took 71 images. After all images are imported into the software, it requires time to calculate the resulting point cloud from the reconstructed camera positions, which allows us to generate the geometry and texture, as we see in Figure 2-11 (which also shows the original statue as an inset on the left).

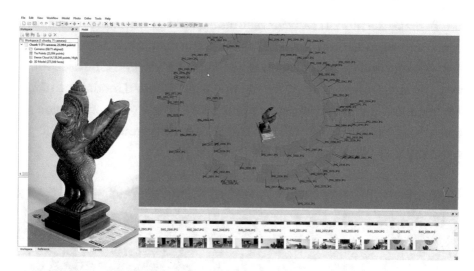

Figure 2-11. *Generating geometry and textures from a photogrammetry point cloud in Agisoft PhotoScan*

As the resulting mesh is close to 300,000 faces, it is important to clean up the geometry as much as possible, delete stray vertices and faces, and close holes in the mesh in Blender (see Figure 2-12).

Figure 2-12. *Cleaning up the high-resolution mesh in Blender*

To make the model ready for real-time graphics, we need to generate a low polygon mesh and bake the high polygon data into a normal map. A very useful and free application called Instant Meshes can be used for that. Instant Meshes analyzes the high-density imported model and offers a number of ways to optimize the topology of the new reduced polygon mesh that it produces. A comb tool allows us to draw guidelines for the geometry flow (see Figure 2-13).

Figure 2-13. *Instant meshes help create low polygon meshes with a good topology flow*

The resulting low polygon mesh as seen in Figure 2-14 is a good base for UV texture mapping and baking.

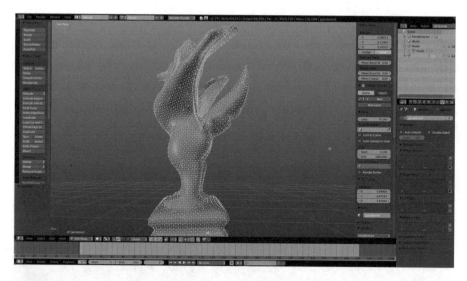

Figure 2-14. *The Instant Meshes low polygon export, reviewed in Blender*

Once the high polygon mesh is baked into a texture set, we can review the result in Marmoset Toolbag's viewer application (see Figure 2-15).

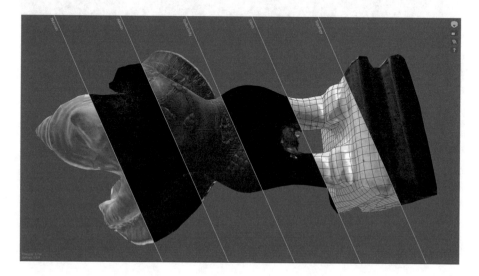

Figure 2-15. *Reviewing the low polygon mesh with the baked texture set*

We are now ready to import all assets into Unreal. In the Material editor, we can experiment with different settings, for example, replacing the roughness and metallic textures with constant values, by holding down the number 1 key on the keyboard and clicking the Material editor. This allows us to input any value between zero and one numerically, as shown in Figure 2-16.

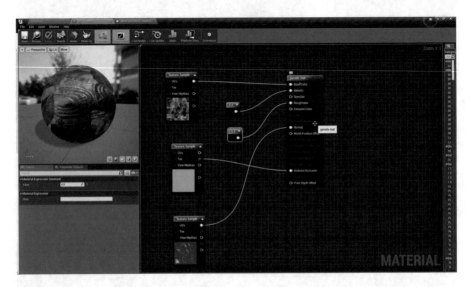

Figure 2-16. *Replacing roughness and metallic textures with constant values*

Opening the color map in the Unreal image viewer allows us to adjust the image values for more realism. As demonstrated in Figure 2-17, the brightness was increased and the saturation reduced.

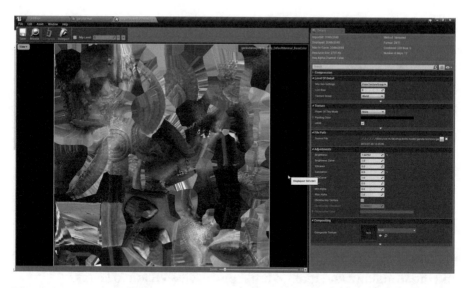

Figure 2-17. *Quick image adjustments on the imported color texture*

The result (see Figure 2-18) is a reasonably good representation of the originally piece, with just a fraction of the size of the original high polygon dataset.

Figure 2-18. *The low polygon Garuda with baked textures from the high polygon model*

37

VR Audio

Audio is one of the most important components in a convincing VR experience. A great number of high-end VR projects put a lot of effort into crafting soundscapes that mirror the VR world and elevate the feeling of presence through sound design.

As a matter of fact, new techniques in VR storytelling have put immersive audio at the center stage of production. For example, a sound from behind can reveal a new story component once the user turns around, and a voice is often used as a navigation assistant.

To unlock the creative power of positional audio in VR, it is important to understand the basic concepts of spatial audio, ambisonic sound design and the workflows and tools to build persuasive VR audio layers.

Using Spatialized Sound

Unreal provides pretty good spatial audio right out of the box. If we open the content examples under the Learn tab in the Epic Games launcher and apply them to a new project, we are able to explore the audio examples from the audio map. Gallery example 1.3 (in Figure 2-19) allows us to explore a spatialized ambient sound and its settings. The details panes on the right show the various available options for spatialized sound, once the Allow Spatialization checkbox is ticked.

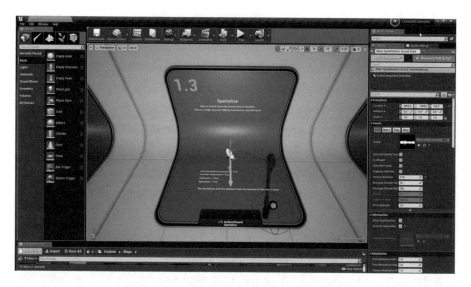

Figure 2-19. *Spatial audio example from the Unreal content examples*

The list of options for spatial audio includes a number of attenuation settings that regulate the distance-based falloff, but also more advanced features such as low-pass filters and occlusion, determining how the sound behaves if objects are between the user and the audio location in the 3D space. For example, if the low-pass filter is enabled, it will interactively be applied when the sound is occluded by an object, simulating real-world frequency response behavior, where higher frequencies are cut off in such a situation.

A typical example is the sound of muffled music in a room next door, where the higher frequencies become clearer the closer and more direct the user is exposed to the sound source. While it is interesting to explore the build-in examples and features for spatial audio in Unreal, we have to be aware that the higher-end features are not available for Android-based mobile and standalone VR headsets right out of the box. Basic directional spatialization with head-related transfer functions (HRTF) is supported, which means sound localization is aided by binaural reproduction.

Typically, we use an ambient background soundscape in conjunction with positional mono sound events that we position in the 3D world according to the event location. For most VR experiences and B2B presentations, this is good enough. But, there are cases where audio plays a center role, as in many AAA games and exploration-type VR gallery and art showcases, where the audio plays a much more prominent and interactive role.

High-End VR Audio with FMOD

For more advanced spatial audio design, including room simulation features such as balanced reflections, we have to turn to third-party software solutions, such as FMOD audio middleware. FMOD integrates with Unreal, and Oculus supports the FMOD Unreal integration with its Oculus Audio Spatializer plugin (see Figure 2-20).

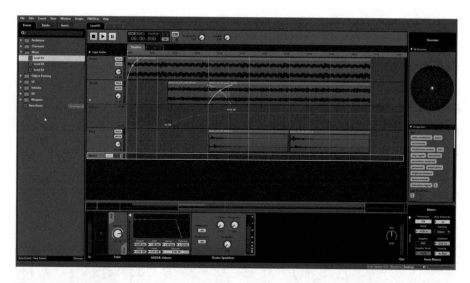

Figure 2-20. *The Oculus Audio Spatializer plugin, applied on the master track in FMOD*

FMOD is free to use for Indie developers and the Oculus integration supports Android mobile and standalone VR, including the Oculus Go. To use it, we need to create an FMOD account and download the application and the plugin for the Unreal integration, which exposes the FMOD features and Blueprints in Unreal. In the next step, we need to download the FMOD plugins from the Oculus developer homepage and move it into the FMOD plugin folder.

In this book, we focus only on the basic spatial audio features that Unreal comes with and not go into the full VR audio pipeline using FMOD and the Oculus Audio SDK, as this would require its own book volume because of the complexity of the subject matter and the large number of development options and production steps.

The Oculus Spatializer VST Plugin for DAWs

Nevertheless, there are tools that provide a good solution for smaller projects that require sound design for VR. One of the other free tools that Oculus provides from the Developer Download page is a virtual studio technology (VST) Spatializer plugin for digital audio workstations (DAW). Typically, using a DAW is the first step in audio design for background tracks, events sounds, and audio loops. Figure 2-21 shows the Oculus Spatializer VST applied to an audio track in Ableton Live, one of the most popular professional audio arrangement tools.

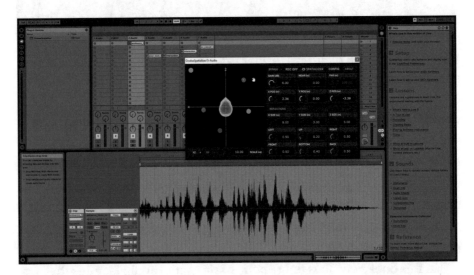

Figure 2-21. *The Oculus Spatializer VST applied as an insert effect on an audio track in Ableton Live*

The VST panel allows you to control each track as individual position in space through the XYZ axis, each represented by a colored dot, in either XZ- or XY-axis view. The resulting mix can then be rendered out as a binaural or ambisonic mix. For sound designers working on a VR project, this is a great way to produce an HRTF-compatible ambisonic mix that responds to the user's head position as part of the virtual reality audio environment.

Why Unreal Is Great for VR Development

We have looked at the 3D asset pipeline for Unreal VR projects and have summarized the audio options that VR developers have using Unreal. Before we dive into more VR specific features, let's take a step back and ask why would we choose to work with Unreal and not any of the other software choices. Obviously, every game engine and VR development platform has its pros and cons, but Unreal is really in a league of its own, for a number of reason that are important to VR development.

Development Scalability with Unreal

First, the scalability of Unreal sets it apart from any other software. Unreal scales up from the single indie developer to a large production of hundreds of team members. In the back of our minds, we know that anytime, when we reach a new development level, or have a surprise hit on our hands that would require a rapid expansion of development operations, the software would be able to keep up.

Hugely successful Unreal titles such as *Gears of War*, *BioShock*, *Mass Effect*, and the megahit *Fortnite* are just a few examples of the impressive AAA lineup pushing the limits of hardware and software. This track record is reflected in the matured toolset, especially when it comes to challenging areas such as character animation, visual effects, and high-quality visualizations, while holding up high frame rates.

A Future-Proof Production Powerhouse

Another reason why Unreal is unbeatable is the fact that developers have full and unrestricted source code access. The typical boutique VR studio, that relies mostly on Blueprints, will not need source code access, but it gives us a peace of mind knowing, that any problem can be solved, if it ever comes down to it. When working in the Unreal editor, there are two areas that stand out: the powerful material and shader system, and the deep integration and flexibility of the Blueprint visual scripting system. The fact that Unreal users enjoy very quick release cycles with bug fixes, feature additions, and improvements makes it exciting to be part of the Unreal community. Each small point release brings so many improvements, that they could qualify as version releases by other software standards.

Specifically in terms of VR development, the company has shown its commitment and dedication to the technology, by its own contributions of VR titles and by the full integration of all the leading VR SDKs, from mobile via standalone to tethered HMDs. When choosing Unreal, you don't have to install an endless number of extensions or plugins for it to be usable. Instead, it already comes as a very complete development platform right out of the box.

In short, it's a good time to be an Unreal VR developer.

VR Best Practices, UX Standards, and Special Areas of Interest

Before we move on to practical hands-on examples, we should quickly examine in the areas that VR differs from other games or interactive media production, the key areas of VR that require extra attention, the established best practices, and how to implement UX conventions.

UI Concepts for the Endless Screen

First, let's talk about screen space. In VR, the user faces an endless screen, and for that reason typical methods of placing user interface (UI) items near the edge of the screen become obsolete as there is no screen edge. As a possible solution for the problem, the interface design takes inspiration from a heads-up display in a visor, which means the UI items are locked to the head's location and rotation. This is referred to as a *non-diegetic* UI. While this solution may work for some projects, especially the ones where the visor is tied in with the storytelling or aesthetics of the subject matter, it may not be appropriate for other situations, where this design choice could come across as too intimidating or too technical, especially where the aesthetics require an open visual space.

Another option is to use spatial design, which means the UI items are placed in the VR world. In many cases, this approach has the advantage that the viewing position can be in a more comfortable mid-view region, or if it is not, the user is able to center his view. If the user has the ability to use free roaming locomotion, he may move into a better position that provides the best viewing distance.

While spatial UI elements are not actually part of the game world, diegetic UI elements are actually part of the VR experience and narrative elements, such as display on a gun, an in-game computer monitor, or TV screen. The fourth UI category to be considered is classified as Meta UI, this method refers to indirect or abstract UI information, for example, when the environment changes color, urging player action.

Spatial and especially diegetic UI concepts are very VR friendly, because the UI is part of the 3D space that the user experiences. It feels natural in VR to activate UI items within objects that are presented within the environment.

Optimizing UI with Curved Elements

Another important consideration when designing UI element for VR is the fact that in VR space most elements are best viewed on curved areas, as on a bent canvas. For example, a large display area in front of the user would be a curved screen, making sure the viewed area maintains a constant distance to the viewer as shown in Figure 2-22.

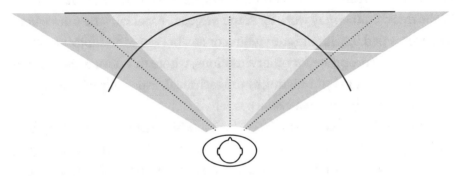

Figure 2-22. *A rounded UI with a continuous viewing distance*

Or, if non-curved elements are placed, they would be arranged in a curved order, with the same goal of achieving equal distance to the user.

VR Locomotion

A much debated subject is locomotion in VR. While teleportation from hotspot to hotspot is an established standard to avoid discomfort and motion sickness in users, there are other alternatives, such as free-roaming locomotion and on-rails-locomotion, to name two. Free-roaming locomotion is mostly used in first-person shooter games and VR experiences that cater to this audience.

On-rails locomotion has a number of variations, and one that has become very popular for mobile and standalone VR is hotspot-activated-rails locomotion. In such a scenario, the user activates the hotspot of the desired location to travel to, and instead of being switched to a new location via teleportation, he travels on an invisible rail from hotspot A to hotspot B, using constant acceleration.

The advantage of this technique is that the experience of traveling through a 3D space enhances the subjective sensation of immersive exploration. It also provides a number of options to design the user experience. By carefully crafting the on-rails path through the VR experience, it is possible to stage graphic highlights and hide areas where graphic detail was reduced, for performance reasons.

Focus on Usability and Core Magic of VR

One key area of designing a VR experience is the motion controller setup. In the current generation of mobile- and standalone VR HMDs, we are dealing with 3DOF (three degrees of freedom) motion controllers, which in most experience function as a laser pointer to activate items. Even though the functions of the controller are limited, there is a wide range of design-driven options to enhance the interaction. We should not forget that what is called "the core magic of VR" happens during the interaction with the immersive world. One example is instead of just interacting with the ray of the motion controller when opening a container, the interaction can be switched to a faded-in animated hand, executing the operation and thereby making the action more dramatic and visually striking.

When assigning the controller buttons, we have to take into consideration how the app will be used. Is it a standing VR experience or a seated one? For some reason, a lot of VR developers assume that the VR experience is done while standing, even though most users use it seated. If the app requires you to constantly turn around in a 360 environment, for example, it excludes users that may want to use the experience on an airplane. Mobility is obviously one of the biggest selling points of mobile and standalone VR and to make the app unusable in a public seating area, such as on an airplane, could be a questionable decision. Developers that consider seated situations very often provide snap rotation on the controller touchpad, an elegant and flexible solution (see the example in Figure 2-23).

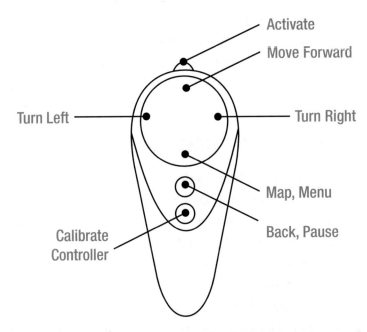

Figure 2-23. *A controller assignment for free movement, used, for example, in The Well, an immersive fantasy RPG for the Oculus Go and Gear VR*

It allows the user to snap his view in 10- to 20-degree increments around his axis in the 360 environment. Some apps have options to disable snap rotation or adjust the speed of it.

VR for B2B Applications

While these options are very often important for the consumer entertainment market, they may be less crucial for typical B2B apps. The bulk of business VR apps are a standing experience, where the presentation is clearly staged in front of the user. Typically, business VR is presented in the booth at a trade show, where a short immersive product introduction is the goal. In these situations, the controller has to be reduced to its most basic function, to avoid confusion for inexperienced casual users.

UX Design for VR

Planning the user experience for a VR experience is where it all comes together. How the UI is laid out, locomotion choices, sound design to assist navigation and the way interaction drives how the storytelling unfolds. An important part of UX is to make the user feel comfortable through anchor objects that help with orientation and that eliminate motion sickness. Next to letting the user ease into the experience, it is also a good practice to have significant pauses between sections of high intensity.

UX Design Methods

Traditional methods of UX design also apply in VR, such as drawing a flowchart that shows the users journey through the experience's options. The old-fashioned whiteboard, or pen and pencil, is a good start before prototyping in 3D. Research and observation is another important part of the process. How do others do it? For an emerging medium as VR that is constantly changing and evolving, UX standards are not set in stone. Instead, they are driven by innovators that are pushing the limits and are constantly refining how to best engage the user. For that reason, it is an important part of the UX design process to evaluate successful titles and to observe audiences' reactions. In short, spend a lot of time in VR and take note of things that work well, that are tackling common problems.

Bringing All Components Together

A satisfying VR experience is built when all pillars are equally strong.

- Optimized graphic assets and environments that provide a rich world without sacrificing performance.

- Sound design that takes advantage of the possibilities in VR to help make the VR world more immersive and help the user orient and navigate.

- A carefully crafted storytelling progression.

- UI elements that are comfortable to use and are, if possible, part of the environment.

- UX design to bring forward the core magic of VR: immersive interaction that leaves the user with the sensation of empowerment.

Conclusion

In this chapter, we looked at the basic workflows to produce content for VR. We evaluated prerendered stereoscopic 360 images as content options when captured from an Unreal environment, and discussed how to preview a VR image sequence on the Oculus Go. In comparison, we went through the steps that a 3D real-time asset requires, such as polygon modeling, unwrapping UV texture coordinates, and reviewing texture layers before importing components into the Unreal Engine and assigning the texture channel in the Material editor.

As an alternative technique, we discussed the photogrammetry pipeline to capture an object with an image sequence and generate a high-resolution mesh with texture that was then transferred to an optimized low polygon model for setup in Unreal. To address the importance of sound in a VR experience, we went over the basic options of spatial sound design and the external tools for production.

And, for preview purposes, we addressed designing sound components with professional digital audio workstations such as Ableton Live.

Finally, this chapter covered the important components that have to be considered when designing for VR: UI, locomotion, interaction, and UX recommendations.

CHAPTER 3

Before You Start

Introduction

In this chapter, we look at all aspects of VR production from a conceptual side. This includes fundamental question on VR as a medium, ways to understand the role of VR opposed to other media types, and the process of bringing ideas into a VR format, including approaches on how to align one's mindset with the technical side, as being productive with visual scripting based on an object-oriented paradigm.

We ask fundamental questions about human perception and how our vestibular system of balance and spatial orientation deals with a simulation situation. And we will look at how stereopsis and perceptual illusion are important to creating a consistent and positive experience that will lead to user retention. We will explore the options to establish an overarching design philosophy and look at potential flaws, vulnerabilities, and blind spots in making design decisions.

Finally, we take a critical look at some of the established best practices and discuss potential shortcomings, workarounds, innovative ideas, considerations of using resources in the most efficient ways, and what areas to focus on.

The Big Picture

Before we get to the hands-on, practical side of building VR interactions in Unreal in the next chapter, let's look at some of the more fundamental questions of a VR project. Starting with these questions: *Why VR? Is VR the*

© Cornel Hillmann 2019
C. Hillmann, *Unreal for Mobile and Standalone VR*,
https://doi.org/10.1007/978-1-4842-4360-2_3

right medium for the project? What actually is VR? What is our core concept, and how will we communicate it?

In a next step, we look at the more conceptual side of the production elements. Before we get our hands dirty with wiring up Blueprint nodes, let's look at the overall architecture of visual scripting from a designer's perspective, and discuss how to best tackle some of its less accessible concepts. The questions here are *How do we translate ideas into Blueprints?* and *How to think like Blueprints?* Looking at design concept options, establishing solutions that help our vision and applying learnings from others to find our own design philosophy will help us answer how to design better, faster, and with higher impact.

The good news is that virtual reality development is still fluid, nothing is yet set in stone, and it is a playground for a lot of disciplines that can give valuable input. Designers, programmers, educators, historians, psychologists, architects, scientists, and writers have contributed VR concepts and ideas and continue to do so. VR is at the forefront of the elements that will shape culture in the years to come, and for that reason, an important stage for interdisciplinary experiments.

Why VR?

It is too easy to overlook the most obvious questions: *Why VR? Does this project have to be in VR? What are the benefits?* To answer these questions, we may want to look at it from a media management perspective. Let's assume we are in charge of the media budget for a new project and have to allocate funds to the different media channels. It is obvious at this point that VR doesn't have the media reach that other formats or channels have (but this will most likely change over time). Nevertheless, good arguments are needed to justify a VR budget that allows a production on a professional level. Luckily, there are enough hard facts, case studies, and success stories to support the notion that VR has a profound impact on users and is a unique way to communicate ideas. The key points are as follows.

- No other medium can evoke empathy as VR does by putting yourself in someone else's shoes.

- No other medium can convey scale as VR does, as traditional media devices are limited by their rectangular frames (see Figure 3-1).

- No other medium gets the uncompromised attention during usage, a fact that troubles a lot of other media types with users having divided attention between a number of screens, such as TV, smartphones, and tablets.

- VR can amplify human intelligence by enhancing pattern recognition in complex data visualization.

- Hardly any other media type is able to evoke a similar sense of marvel and wonder with its interactions in 3D space, presence and spatial exploration as VR does. The user perceives it as magic if done well.

Figure 3-1. *Experiencing scale in VR (image by C. Hillmann)*

This means if we are planning a project where any of these five qualities—empathy, scale, attention, complexity, magic—plays a role, then we already have a strong proposition for the usage of VR, as there are proven use cases for it.

But before getting ahead of ourselves, we should also ask a few critical questions. If VR has these unique qualities, why is the adoption rate not much higher? Let's use a typical example to illustrate this question. Anecdotal evidence suggests that first-time users are very often amazed by their first exposure to a VR experience, but when asked if inclined to come back or purchase a headset, the response is typically along the lines of, *It's amazing, but I've seen enough of it.*

Let's try to understand this user behavior. The exposed user confirmed the extraordinary value of a VR experience, but there is an obstacle to evoke a desire of repeating it. This problem has long been part of the heated discussion around the issues of consumer adoption. In this discussion, we have various camps. One position is that the technical hurdles and the high price are holding people back. Another camp, including the notable voice of Oculus founder Lucky Palmer, questions this position with the statement that the quality of VR hardware and software is not yet good enough for a mass market. Better resolution and ergonomics, and deeper content addressing a wider variety of users, would be needed.

No matter which camp is right, either problem is a temporary one, and as quality, ergonomics and price issues get resolved over time, the market will move from enthusiasts and early adopters to a broader audience.

But within this discussion there is also a possible third problem that may easily be overlooked. The notion that the desire for immersion could actually be a matter of personal preference. In the VR mass-adoption discussion, it is mostly assumed that immersive media is the natural successor of framed media, labeling all dives with rectangular screens as such. This idea is based on a linear projection of consumer behavior. The obvious evidence for this assumption would be the observation that consumers would always get the next bigger TV once the price is right. In this linear projection, a hypothetical future TV would almost entirely wrap around the consumer possibly with a motion-tracking interface, which comes close to what VR delivers.

But instead of assuming that this projection is a fact, it is also legitimate to question it. There is a possibility that a percentage of consumers prefer not to be immersed, no matter how good or affordable it is. Anecdotal evidence suggests that there is a percentage of people who feel uncomfortable being immersed in a simulated artificial environment. People with this preference would always choose a framed media device over an immersive one, at least in the current media environment.

This observation plays into the hands of AR developers, who are betting on a future where simulations are embedded in the actual environment as overlays to reality. But, let's not forget that these strict differentiations are also most likely only temporary. A realistic expectation of a XR future includes the seamless transitions between AR and VR. A user may have an AR device casually running while relaxing, but may switch to a VR view if seeing something interesting that needs to be explored in detail.

VR will always be the richer and more complete simulation experience than any AR solution will ever be able to deliver, but AR may be the entry point for consumers in a future mixed-reality environment. What it comes down to is the observation that consumers that feel uncomfortable diving into a simulation will most likely have less objections in an environment that allows the transition into the simulation, and back, be smoother and more elegant, in an ideal case scenario supported by a technical infrastructure of familiar and social components.

Coming back to the original question, why VR? VR is an investment in the future—on the company level as well as on the personal level. This investment is not only the actual production, but also the learnings and the understandings of the wider implications that reveal themselves in the process.

What Is VR Anyway?

It may be surprising for the casual observer to see the number of active online discussions on what VR is and isn't, even after the wider field of immersive media has been sufficiently mapped in widely publicized reference articles and decades of academic research.

The tone of consumer discussions very often tend to sway between emotional and aggressive and is typically between 360 VR video advocates and owners of high-end tethered VR HMDs. A similar disagreement often erupts between owners of 3DOF headsets and 6DOF headsets.

Is 360 VR video and 3DOF not really VR—as very often stated with conviction in consumer discussion forums? Obviously, these are all different variations of VR. The better question to differentiate is, *Is it room-scale VR?* Room-scale VR is only limited to 6DOF headsets, and at this point, not fully possible with VR video (with the exception of volumetric video). Of course, a 3DOF HMD cannot do room scale, but is obviously VR per definition.

The definition of what VR is has matured over decades. The academic definition can be summarized in a short sentence. VR is the interaction with an artificial environment. That includes early VR installations, such as cave systems, where wall projections were used as a simulation environment and at first pioneered in flight simulators. The line of what VR is and what it is not can be drawn at immersive viewing devices.

View-Master, the classic stereoscopic toy (see Figure 3-2) launched in the 1960s as a device for viewing popular cartoon and film scenes in 3D. It is not a VR device. It can be called a predecessor to VR, but per definition, the device is not virtual reality because there is no interaction with the viewed imagery.

Figure 3-2. *Viewmaster (1966), a stereoscopic viewer, but not a VR device (CC0, courtesy Wikipedia)*

Any viewing device that is headlocked to the viewer cannot be called VR. Interaction starts with the free head movement that allows you to change the viewing angle toward the environment. VR is when the user interacts with the environment.

That is why 360 VR video is indeed a form of VR, whereby the user can move his head, and by doing so is interacting with the environment; whereas the original View-Master was a great stereoscopic immersive viewing device, but not a VR device. The same can be said for a number of so-called personal viewing headsets that are headlocked and meant to be TV-movie screen alternatives. And, even though a lot of 360 videos are of poor quality, low resolution, and very often not even stereoscopic, they fulfill the definition of VR. Once a device or experience is classified as VR, there are enormous differences in the quality and scope of interaction, including room-scale up to arena-scale abilities, as demonstrated with the Oculus Quest.

Breaking Down Reality

To better understand what virtual reality does to the human mind, let's look at how sensory input is utilized to experience one's surroundings and what elements drive the complex ideas of subjective reality that the human brain uses to create its idea of the outer world.

A fascinating cultural arc was established with one of the early virtual reality cave experiments in 1992 at the Electronic Visualization Laboratory (EVL) at the University of Illinois in Chicago by referencing the allegory of the cave from Plato's Republic (see Figure 3-3).

Figure 3-3. *Bust of Plato, author of The Republic in 380 BC (CC0, courtesy Pixabay)*

Plato's cave allegory is one of the most profound pieces of western philosophy and touches fundamental questions of perception and the nature of reality. In essence, it describes a situation in which people in a cave can only see shadows, without knowing the origin of the shadows and how they are projected. They accept the shadows as living entities and part of reality until, one day, it is learned that the shadows are actually only projections of entities outside. By learning that, a concept of constructed reality is shattered, and insight is gained in that what has been accepted as reality was a reflection of the more complex system that produced it. With his allegory, Plato is asking questions on our perception of reality, the fundamentally subjective nature of perception, the hidden nature of reality, the role of illusion, and the limits of our senses.

All of these are questions that are relevant in a larger discourse on virtual reality. In a way, the cave's wall shadows were a form of virtual reality for its observers. We could even say that in its profound symbolism, Plato foreshadowed the discussion about the role of virtual reality in society. Reaching into cultural and historical parallels and referencing ancient ideas have been an accompanying feat of VR development subtext led by a league of VR thinkers since its emergence from the subcultures of the 1980s and '90s. It is a showcase of how culture and technology can create a powerful feedback loop, bridging eternal questions of the existence, medium, and perception over centuries, and thus touching and refining the core of the human experience.

The backdrop of a cultural-technological discourse can be helpful in creating innovation impulses. It is one of the tools that help innovators to think outside of the box, and by looking at the larger historical perspective, filter out the important questions that need to be solved.

On a mere practical level, the VR cave experiments and Plato's allegory bring up question that are actually quite insightful when looking at VR development. What is needed to make the world believable? What sensory input is essential in conveying a real world. And opposite of that, what can we get away with? What will the user accept as reality without breaking immersion.

It is very often surprising how much the human mind is willing to accept a new reality and its rules. Just as Plato's cave shadows were accepted as the real thing, so can simplified artificial environment be accepted as real, as long as the rules are believable, consistent, and reliable.

Reconstructing Reality

Understanding how input creates an internal mental model of reality is key in establishing the factors that are essential for a successful simulation. The consciousness is always lagging behind perception trying to recognize patterns and filling in the gaps to complete them. Pointers create expectations and the mind fills the gaps with imagination, even with the most abstract shapes, forms, and stimuli.

The internal mental model builds expectations about how the world behaves and interacts. The scholar Alfred Korzybski (1879–1950) once coined the phrase, "The map is not the territory." The map stands for the subjective reality, the mental model that we create of reality by our beliefs, filters, expectations, and assumptions. As Korzybski defined it, human knowledge is limited by language and the nervous system, thus having no direct access to reality.

If we look at the construction of reality from this particular angle, we may want to approach the general philosophy of VR world-building by starting with a void space and evaluating what components are most essential to build a sustainable framework for the mind to operate in.

Let's assume a mind experiment in which our short- and mid-term memory has been completely erased, and we wake up in a desert. The first questions that pop into our minds are, *Where am I, and how did I get here? What am I doing here?* Our eyes scan the environment for hints and familiar items.

Until we find something to hold on to, and until it is able to lock down the situation, the brain is basically in panic mode.

From a VR developer's perspective, this thought experiment has an important message: the human mind wants to be comforted. Let's throw it a bone. Show the user a familiar item. As quickly as possible, let the user know where he is, at what scale, what his role is, and what his purpose is in this reality. Let's give the user hints and early guidance of what kind of world this is and what he can expect. Let's give him pointers, style references, and content hints.

The human mind wants to feel safe and in control and by giving the necessary guidance we can evoke that very feeling. That is why a lot of experiences start with a computer desk in VR. A familiar setting is comforting, and little hints in the environment can be absorbed piece by piece to grasp what world this is. The gradual introduction into the VR world is of elemental importance.

The early introduction UX is a make or break in many cases. It is creating the initial stage for building engagement, and that includes rewarding attentional gaze, interacting with visual cues in the virtual environments, supporting wayfinding aids with audio, and adding color to emphasize reactions.

Core Concept and GDD

Traditionally, game productions, including VR projects, are documented in the game design document (GDD) which covers all aspect of the production from backstory to game mechanics to characters and individual assets. The document is the foundation for sharing the overall concept and defines the scope of the endeavor, which allows cost estimates and man hours by itemizing tasks and assets.

The GDD is obviously not only good for games, but the foundation for any complex interactive media production, including educational or enterprise VR. As a living design document, it provides the guiding vision for all participants: artists, designers, programmers, management, and partners. It is to some part the equivalent of what in broadcast and film the production bible is, but due to the highly technical nature of entertainment software development, it breaks down distinct program areas and procedures, including features and functions.

GDDs are part of the game development culture, and because of the long history and well-documented examples, they can be a great resource for learning. The easiest way is to start with a template from one of the

many sites that offer them for free. Game development sites such as
Gamasutra.com have a lot of resources on all angles of GDD creation.
A well-done GDD can be a piece of art; some actually are, for example,
when the overall presentation is designed like brand manual with care for
detail and careful choices for icons and fonts.

In the end, it is the document that sells the project concept, not only
to partners for funding, but also to each team member and collaborator.
When an original game mechanic concept is presented, artistic sketches
and powerful concept art motivate everyone involved to bring the ideas
to life. In that sense, a GDD is also a motivational instrument, the vision
keeper's bible and propaganda pamphlet.

Concept art plays a big role in a GDD. It is the visual introduction to the
ideas in it, and it is very often the first thing that sticks when flipping through it.

There is an incredible production value in having the core concepts
sketched out as striking concept art.

Exciting concept art lifts a technical document from being mere
production guidelines to a dynamic call for action. Concept art on a more
abstract level (see Figure 3-4) leaves room for imagination and can be an
instrument of accelerating the creative process.

Figure 3-4. *Abstract concept art (image by C. Hillmann)*

While concept art that shows late-stage 3D visualization convey progress in a GDD (see Figure 3-5).

Figure 3-5. *3D concept visualization (image by C. Hillmann)*

It communicates that the project is already underway. A good GDD evokes excitement, through visual art, original ideas, and well-executed technical documentation. If a team is good at producing a tight GDD, they will most likely be good in production, as well.

There are a good number of GDDs from famous games available online as public resources. They are very often interesting to study in comparison to the final product and often have witty to quirky to fun details to offer. A GDD for a VR project should bring up the crucial VR topics right up front and should devote locomotion, UI, and distinct VR mechanics before getting into the level details, this way the document's unique VR features can easily be isolated and pinpointed, as part of the core concept.

A GDD also addresses the market situation and defines the target audience. It is most of the time the first step in a project development, followed by a prototype or a more elaborate vertical slice.

The Object-Oriented Mindset: Converting Ideas into Blueprints

When looking at the conceptual side of development for VR, it is important to look at the possible technical obstacles and the best strategies to implement game mechanic concepts into performance-optimized functions. This book is primarily addressing VR developers that come from a non-coding design background. Typically, this would cover not only multimedia designers, CG artists, and 3D creators, but also technical artists coming from other areas of media development. For example, for a CG artist from a DCC software such as Maya, 3D Studio Max, or Blender, it takes a bit of time and understanding of some of the foundations that Unreal Blueprint is based on.

The Blueprint visual scripting system in Unreal is very accessible. As a matter of fact, some of the most basic procedures are easy to grasp with common sense and universal logical thinking. Basic branch operations based on boolean variables, such as *If this is true, then this happens*, have an inherent logic that stands on its own.

On the other hand, due to its C++ nature, operations that are strongly tied to the object-oriented paradigm that Unreal is based on may not be immediately obvious to a person coming from a DCC package. For example, a technical artist working in Maya using MEL script is used to having all scene objects available at all times when referencing them in a script. As long as the object lives in the world, it can be referenced directly, including all of its parameters.

The object-oriented programming environment (the paradigm behind Unreal's Blueprint system) is a bit of a different animal. Newcomers very often struggle with the concept of inheritance and encapsulation. These two concepts are, next to polymorphism and abstraction, two of the four basic concepts of the object-oriented principles, where the structure of the language's foundation is based on objects rather than actions (see Figure 3-6).

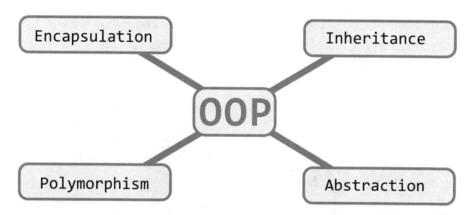

Figure 3-6. *Object-oriented programming principles (image by C. Hillmann)*

The concepts are very obvious and omnipresent in Unreal Blueprints. Inheritance becomes immediately obvious with the parent and child classes in Blueprints, such as the character class which is a child of the pawn class, so it inherits its attributes. Encapsulation is probably the concept that troubles newcomers the most, as you cannot directly reference variables in a different actor class. Instead, you need to reference the targeted class through its hierarchy. Typically, this is done with a reference using the *cast to* node.

Encapsulation is basically hiding the values of structured data objects inside of a class, preventing direct access, thus preserving its integrity, but also making it more difficult to work with it.

It is a good idea to read up on the basic concepts of object-oriented programming vs. functional or procedural programming to get an idea of what the purpose and advantage of this approach is. Requiring only a minimal time investment, reading the public online references, starting with Wikipedia, gives any Blueprint user a good head start in understanding the basic foundations without having to learn any C++ in depth (see Figure 3-7).

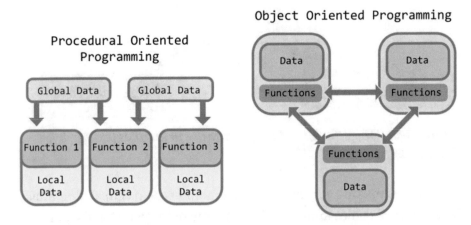

Figure 3-7. *Comparing procedural-oriented programming to object-oriented programming (image by C. Hillmann)*

In this context, it is interesting to learn that not everyone is in love with object-oriented programming (OOP). For example, one common criticism addresses the overhead of dealing with class inheritance in OOP. Joe Armstrong, the creator of the Erlang language, once famously said about OOP, *You wanted a banana, but what you got was a gorilla holding the banana and the entire jungle.*

A widely circulated *Medium* article titled "Goodbye, Object-Oriented Programming" goes through all the issues with OOP. Marc Flurry, the co-creator of the famous hit title *Thumper*, dismissed OOP in his 2017 GDC talk, "Seven Years in Alpha: The Thumper Postmortem." With this discussion, it becomes clear that OOP is not for everyone and every situation. For example, a small coder-artist team, such as the team behind *Thumper*, in their own unique process, was most likely more dynamic and flexible without it.

Following debates and discussion like this gives interesting insights, and sharpens the perception of best practices and use cases.

Unreal's Blueprint system uses only a basic subset of the object oriented paradigm, thanks to that it avoids most of the pitfalls and complexity mentioned earlier.

Overall, there is no question that the Unreal Blueprint system is an efficient and powerful tool to create interactive systems. The object-oriented paradigm is fully aligned with the inherent structure of game design, by which functions are assigned to game objects. Blueprints have a clear language that is unobstructed and clearly structured. The high degree of consistency, its coherent UI, and the accessibility due to its visual nature is unparalleled. For visual artists, Blueprints are a godsend.

In Chapter 4, we look at the event graph of a level Blueprint. The level Blueprint is the only Blueprint that allows easy direct access to all actors placed in the level, but unlike class Blueprints, it cannot be inherited and is level specific. Due to its unique quality of easy access to all actors, it is very often the best introduction to someone coming from a visual arts field, as it can be compared to a large canvas where relationships and interactions between level actors can be established and designed. The level Blueprint can also be seen as a playground to test ideas in the open, without having to store events and functions away in a separate Blueprint class, which adds an additional layer of abstraction and extra work to access them. The level Blueprint was actually the predecessor to Blueprints, where the visual scripting system Kismet in Unreal Engine 3 had its origin.

In the later chapters, we move away from the level Blueprint and increasingly build events in our actor classes. This has the advantage of being independent of a level and having modular reusable object that can function in any environment, as it has its events and functions encapsulated. The better we understand the benefits of OOP as it is reflected in the usage of Blueprints, the easier it is for us to express ideas in it.

The Blueprint Dev Journal

It is highly recommended to maintain a Blueprint development journal. It is easy to explain why. Typically, we run into similar problems at every new project setup. A number of standard procedures such as setting up teleportation, basic controller functions, and object interaction follow a similar pattern, while they may differ slightly in each particular case and project.

It is a good idea to keep a reference with a screenshot and a description of what is happening in that Blueprint screenshot in a development journal. The description should be in plain English, so it easy to grasp at a later point what the flow, intention, and context of that Blueprint was. Using this method, we can easily access solutions that we created in the past at any later point.

A typical case scenario is when working on a complex Blueprint solution and realizing that we had a similar case in the past but don't remember exactly how it was put together. In cases like this, it is a huge time-saver to be able to go back in time using the journal and recapping the previous solution. For most people, a common way to learn is by watching tutorial videos. In the specific case of Blueprints, it can be very tedious to find the right spot in a video where a Blueprint was actually finalized, and when the video position is found, the contextual information is missing. That's why videos or video links are really not the right way to store reference information for quick access at a later point.

The better, more productive way is to keep track of Blueprint solutions in a development journal, where each section contains a screenshot and an explanation of what is happening in it, including intention, context and descriptions of the execution flow.

A development journal is a personal account of learnings and insights that need to be preserved for productivity reasons. We are basically building a house of knowledge, but that also means we have to make sure its foundations are solid and well grounded.

Design Decisions

Let's look at some fundamental design decisions that will determine the conceptual integrity of a VR project. The decisions determine the basic foundations in terms of interaction, locomotion, and style. It's a good idea to take into account what we know so far about user behavior in VR. Let's not forget that research on human interaction in VR goes back into the late 1980s and early '90s. That means there is a lot of knowledge, research data, and experience to draw from, even though the new generation of VR solutions has been able to leapfrog some of the inherent issues that have plagued previous iterations of VR through its technical breakthroughs.

Learning from Illusionists

When approaching VR design decision, it helps to understand the techniques of an illusionist. An illusionist is the master of directing the attention of his audience; he uses tricks and disguises to make believe and to lure the attention away from technical tricks that would give his illusions away. Directing attention is crucial in a VR experience. Research data has shown how users constantly search and scan the environment in an artificial surrounding. By searching, the user is actively pursuing stimuli in his sensory world. Extensive experiments using eye tracking have been conducted to record attention maps showing how users search and scan environments and images.

Typically, the studies offer interesting insights on how the scanning data differ by gender, age, ethnicity, or cultural context. VR world builders are able to learn from these studies, that the search for stimuli can be directed with multisensory clues, along with a variation based on the expectation of the target audience. Visual or audio hints feed directly into the human need to find direction and purpose in his environment.

Doing this consistently, starting at the early stage, allows you to direct the viewer's attention to the high production value of the scene and away from the possible weaker parts of the environment. Hyperbolically speaking, we don't want the user to stare at a random environment prop and say, "Hey, wait a minute. You mapped an image to a polygon, and you want me to believe that this is an actual object?"

In short, the goal is to direct the user's attention and keep him deeply engaged until he is in the flow of the moment, which is a precondition for user retention.

Let's look at some of the other fundamental design elements that can drive a positive user experience.

Audio: The Low-Hanging Fruit

High-quality voice acting and audio design can add a tremendous production value to a VR project, most likely at a lower cost than most of the environment, assets, and animation production. As a self-contained media layer with less scene dependencies than 3D items, it is also easier to handle during a production. On top of that, performance issues play practically no role at all. There are numerous examples, especially from experimental VR creators, VR art installations, and educational titles, where the high-quality audio narration carried the majority of the VR experience.

Specific game genres, such as horror and comedy, are very voice-acting friendly. Voice acting has become extremely accessible through online services such as Voices.com. The production workflow is straightforward and transparent: list a job, including the script, audition, and possible candidates; hire the right talent; and download the completed recording. Compared to the major and costly endeavors this was not too long ago— hiring a studio and advertising for talent and a producer, voice acting has become a well-oiled machine that is now accessible even to smaller productions on a limited budget.

Next to spatial event sounds that are activated at the world coordinates in the Unreal level, ambient audio environment design has a high impact on how the user perceives a scene. There are a number of popular tools that allow you to premix an ambisonic environment.

In addition to the sophisticated toolset from Oculus, which we discussed briefly in Chapter 2, we have third-party options. One example is the Ambisonic Toolkit (`www.ambisonictoolkit.net`) for the low-cost digital audio workstation Reaper. The spatial composition soundfield produced with these tools can be used with the Oculus Audio SDK that is integrated in Unreal.

The Other Low-Hanging Fruit: Consistent Depth Levels

A VR scene really comes to life when all three depth levels—background, middleground, and foreground—are well balanced. Stereo perception tapers off at about 20 meters, so anything beyond that is the background. Items between 5 and 15 meters away can be considered middleground, while items closer than 5 meters are foreground. The 3D stereo perception is the strongest in the foreground with items less than 5 meters away.

A good balance between these three levels results in a very rich and satisfying experience of the 3D world. The opposite, for example, a VR scene without a foreground object, appears less compelling to the user. It is a good idea to try maintaining these three levels throughout the experience's environments to avoid losing the user's attention. For example, a section in the GDD can be devoted to the direction of depth levels, possibly with check marks under each new environment section of the scene, to make sure the depth levels are maintained.

Paying attention to the consistency of depth level, by arranging props and environment composition in alignment with the overall art direction, is an easy way to create a better visual impact and a higher user satisfaction without too much technical effort.

Easy Wins

Very often, an easy way to do improvement of a VR scene is by making it a bit darker to avoid flicker. Instead of setting a VR scene at a full-on bright sunlight, it pays off to move it to a late-afternoon lighting condition. Color management is easier; flicker with contrasting elements can be better contained.

Keeping the experience short, or breaking it up into shorter segments, is a good way to retain the user. Most users prefer shorter experiences. In the current state of VR, mobile, and standalone VR is primarily used as a short break or a quick escape.

Planning well-thought-out constraints is one more way to make a developer's life easier and to keep the user from getting frustrated. Built-in constraints concern often movement and navigation. Naturally, walled off parts of the environment, such as areas behind a cliff, rift, river, fence or barrier, communicate clearly which areas are accessible and which are off limits. Implementing constraints goes way beyond movement and environment and can include UI interaction and motion controller range. It functions as an aid to the user experience, by excluding unnecessary, distracting, confusing, or potentially frustrating elements from the user.

Dealing with Simulation Sickness

VR simulation sickness, often loosely labeled as motion sickness, is a major topic with ongoing research and innovation updates both in hardware and software development. Let's look at the problem and evaluate the degree to which it affects us in the mobile and standalone VR space. Simulator sickness primarily occurs when the apparent or perceived motion is misaligned with the actual physical motion, resulting in discomfort and nausea. What are the typical case scenarios and how can we deal with the problem?

Case number one: the primary and worst case of simulation sickness is caused by latency and bad calibration. An underpowered smartphone with a demanding Gear VR title resulting in frame stutter, frame tearing, and lag while moving the head is probably the worst VR experience one can have. The user's sensory input is under permanent attack, trying to cope with the situation. This simulation sickness scenario is the worst possible offender of any VR situations and should be avoided at all cost. This can easily be done by following best practices, performance guidelines and by correctly profiling the app. Bad hardware calibration can be incorrect IPD settings, but also include bad strappings of the headset without instructions, for example, when done at a public demonstration showcase with first-time users.

Case number two: first-time users often state, "It makes me sick," especially in standalone tethered VR setups. Anecdotal evidence suggests that this expression is more or less a summary of all the discomforting factors that contribute to an unpleasant experience. A casual first-time user may not be able to pinpoint exactly what it was that caused the discomfort, or lacks the technical vocabulary to label the specific item, such as screen door effect, low resolution, headset weight, restricted movement, or even concerns over the hygiene of the used gear, on top of a general bias against immersion, as discussed in the beginning of this chapter.

Very often, the expression *it makes me sick* is the sum of all negative factors and not an actual feeling of nausea. This may have been misinterpreted by researchers as a result of VR locomotion; it actually may be a lot more than that.

Case number three: VR locomotion can indeed lead to simulation sickness in a percentage of the population. Cybersickness is the result of a misalignment between virtual motion and actual physical motion that causes people sensitive to the misalignment to feel nausea.

Because VR has had a long history in scientific laboratories and military research facilities, data and insight on simulation sickness studies are publicly available. Surprisingly, research shows that simulation sickness is very often only a temporary phenomenon, because the body adapts after a short period of time.

A 2005 report on simulator sickness research by the U.S. Army Research Institute for the Behavioral and Social Sciences concluded that only 3% to 5% of individuals never adapt after initial problems, and therefore have a permanent simulation sickness problem. The report states that for the remaining majority of the population, "Adaptation is the single most effective solution." These findings are in dire contrast to the numbers that have otherwise been circulated in media reports, where it was stated that 25% to 40% of consumers have a motion sickness problem. These often published and quoted numbers leave out the important fact that for most individuals, the simulator sickness problem is only a temporary one, and as scientific research has shown, is a matter of adaptation. The report states that most individuals adapt within a few sessions.

We should also take into consideration that adaptation happens not only on the individual level, but also on a broader cultural level, when a society adopts a new technology. Anyone familiar with gaming history may know that when *Doom* was released in 1993, it caused a wave of motion sickness concerns. Players were quoted that the high degree of realism combined with the fast motion caused serious sickness and nausea. It was a widely reported cause for concern back then. Today, first-person shooter (fps) games are mainstream entertainment activity with hundreds of millions of players.

One could even go as far as comparing the phenomenon to the growing pains of technical innovation in previous historical eras. In the 19th century, the introduction of trains replacing horse-driven carriages as means of transportation was a cause for massive concerns and anxieties that the speed of the new technology would cause sickness, mental illness, or raging madness, and would be especially harmful to women. History has shown that anxieties over new technologies are very often inflated and that humans adapt much better and faster than often expected (see Figure 3-8).

Figure 3-8. *Motion sickness hysteria in the 19th century (CC0, courtesy publicdomainpictures.net)*

To sum it up, simulation sickness is a serious problem for a small minority of the population, but for everyone else, including the users that have an initial reaction of simulation sickness, it may be a matter of adoption and a matter of a well-designed user experience that helps to bridge the initial irritation with additional options to help them with the transition.

Over time, simulation sickness concerns in VR led to the universally accepted best-practice rule, that teleportation should be the way of moving around in a virtual reality environment. As these rules were decided at developer conferences and within industry bodies, a gap or disconnect to the hardcore VR gaming crowd became obvious. A large fraction of VR gamers cherished the traditional fps movement, very often called *smooth locomotion,* and was unwilling to accept teleportation as the universal standard.

A grassroots rebellion became obvious in online forums and social media groups. The voices of the VR teleportation resistance had good reasons: a lot of a game is lost in some titles when no free movement is possible. The success story of modern fps gaming is to a great degree owed to the free movement through 3D space. Only by moving through a 3D environment can the actual space be experienced.

Teleportation removed this essential pillar of the gaming experience, making it static and uninteresting for the fps gaming crowd. This resulted in a new and celebrated generation of VR titles that ignored the best-practice guides, and instead offered traditional smooth locomotion as the way to move. After the initial struggle with user preferences and demands, developers have learned and now very often offer options to both, which is clearly the best approach. That way, a new user can use teleportation until feeling more comfortable and at a later point may switch over to smooth locomotion. Giving VR users options has become the new golden rule (see Figure 3-9).

Figure 3-9. *Offering user options to switch between different forms of locomotion: smooth locomotion to teleportation (top), on-rails locomotion (bottom) (image by C. Hillmann)*

These options also depend on what audience a title addresses. An action fantasy game will certainly profit from locomotion options, while for learning, marketing, or enterprise VR apps, teleportation is really the only thing that makes sense. Besides having to decide between smooth locomotion and teleportation, or offering both options, developers have also used alternative locomotion styles, such as vehicle-based, rail-guided, or hovering drone-based movement, allowing for smooth navigation framed with stabilizing cockpit elements. The cockpit remains one of the most comfortable VR settings as it conveys safety, visually stabilizes, and allows constant depth levels. Adding stable visual cues to environments on all depth levels, including a rest frame background, has been one of the most successful recipes against simulator sickness.

Essentials: Snap Rotation

One of the most important considerations for a VR developer is how, where, and by whom the VR application will be used. One of the earliest best-practice rules has always been to never break immersion. This caused VR developers to stay away from snap rotating the view as an immersion breaker. That iron rule has led to the assumption that every user will experience a VR app standing up or using a swivel chair, as a lot of VR experiences require turns to continue.

The reality is that the majority of users prefer a comfortable couch seating, or enjoy a VR app while traveling, for example, in an airplane seat. In common situations, it is not physically possible to turn around, so VR apps requiring it become unusable.

Snap rotation is an essentially important function that every app should have, or at least should offer as an option in the user preferences. Typically, it is mapped to the motion controller's left and right touchpad buttons. Snap rotation is an essential feature that is in line with what users actually do. A good example of excellent user choices is the Oculus Go and

Gear VR title *The Well*, which allows the user to tweak the speed of snap rotation and locomotion in the Options menu, thereby letting the user decide what is best for him.

Unless a VR app is designed to be always forward facing, as some on-rail-based action titles are, snap rotation is a basic ingredient to the set of navigation controls. If a VR app doesn't have it, it is incomplete and will result in user frustration because it is unusable in many typical situations.

Move Fast and Break Things, Including the Rules of VR

While it is a good idea to first internalize the best practices of VR and understand the reasoning behind them, and to evaluate the user benefits and learn from the experience that other successful VR projects have to offer, it can also be beneficial to occasionally question rules to break them intelligently. Mark Zuckerberg once famously stated, "Move fast and break things," encouraging agile development and unconventional thinking.

What are some of the rules that may have been questioned occasionally? Here are a few possible ones in random order:

- Presence is everything.

- Never break immersion.

- Avoid motion sickness at all cost.

These rules have been established for good reasons. Presence is the moment when a VR world becomes so real that you feel you are there. It is the ultimate goal of any VR endeavor. Immersion breaks when something that is not aligned with the perception occurs, which obviously should be avoided. Motion sickness is a major concern because a lot of people experience it initially, and it has to be taken into consideration when designing any sort of VR movement.

Rules can be broken if there is a good reason for it. If we look at the golden rule to never break immersion, which was the reasoning behind not offering snap rotation in a lot of VR applications, we learn that this precaution may have been overreaching. The old argument was that an unnatural movement, such as snap rotation, destroys the user's immersive illusion of being there. Not offering snap rotation has become widely adopted for the fear of breaking immersion and disorienting the user. As it turns out, this fear overshot a concept that is not aligned with what users actually want and experience. Snap rotation is not breaking immersion; instead, it is an important navigation tool that every VR app should have— at least as an option.

The human mind is highly adaptable and quickly adjusts to snap rotation. It adapts and accepts snap rotation as part of the world's inherent rules and mechanics.

Since the early days of the Oculus DK1, some of the most popular VR crowd-pleasers have been VR roller-coaster rides in all variations. Very often snubbed by the development community as a simplistic low-brow phenomenon or ugly stepchild of the otherwise high ambitions for VR entertainment, it is notable that VR roller-coasters and their conceptual evolutions continue to top the charts as the most popular apps. Roller-coaster apps are very often the first exposure that users have, especially with mobile VR, and are typically used as a way to introduce friends to VR by aiming for the maximum impact of an immersive simulation with a familiar hook.

The relentless popularity of roller-coasters and related genres do put into question the third VR rule, to avoid motion sickness at all cost. In a way, it is a complete reversal of that idea. Can motion sickness be a sought-after quality by thrill-seekers? This idea is actually not too farfetched; for example, social situations in which a headset is passed around among a small gathering of friends, where the goal is to test your limits to entertain the group, are proof of that. Could it be that motion sickness is a feature and not a bug? That probably stretches this notion a bit too far, considering the overall diversity of users and applications, but the takeaway is that rules have to be seen in context of the target audience, and where and how it is used, instead of being blindly followed.

Beware of Cheap Thrills

VR roller-coasters bring up the subject of cheap thrills, as there are a few of them and some may be tempting. But, as with overly sweet candy, the effects quickly wear off and leave the user dissatisfied if there is no substance otherwise. VR roller-coasters have an analogy in the physical world, so they are a legit use case, but the danger is that the focus on the acceleration thrill reduces the perception of what VR is to a simplistic experience, while the real wonder and its potential is not presented (see Figure 3-10).

Figure 3-10. *Birthplace of the VR roller-coaster: the Oculus development kit 1 in 2013 (image by C. Hillmann)*

Among the cheap VR thrills, we will also find the jumpscare as a prime example of an overly simplistic way to provoke a user reaction. It is worth noting that VR jumpscares carry an additional and severe stress-burden that is not present in film jump-scares. The added stress-level through jumpscares in a VR horror experience is so dramatic that, very often, even seasoned genre fans prefer not to be exposed to them.

While a VR jumpscare would for sure impress the user, the question is whether the experience was enjoyable and if there is a willingness from the user to come back for more. Any superficial effects that solely rely on accelerated and exaggerated motion and visual disruptions could be considered a breach of trust, as the user has committed in good faith to the exposure of an immersive simulation. Either way, the user has to be informed upfront of the disruptions he can expect and the negative reactions he may have to deal with.

Lessons from the Uncanny Valley

"The uncanny valley" is the descriptive term for humanoid 3D characters aiming to be as realistic as possible, but by being so, invoke a feeling of creepiness and rejection in the audience or user. The problem has been studied thoroughly in context of computer graphics and robotics. Famous examples triggered a public debate on character simulation and its impact on the entertainment industry. The performance capture of the actor Tom Hanks for the CGI motion picture *Polar Express* is an historic example in a heated debate and overwhelming rejection of the results. In the gaming world, the problem is acknowledged, but gamers in general accept it as a trade-off for the benefits of interactive action and storytelling.

Even though the uncanny valley deals explicitly with the acceptance of artificial characters, the broader lesson to be learned for VR development is that the harder we try to create a hyperrealistic world, the more we are prone to fail. The human eye gets increasingly critical if presented with hyperrealism and may deliberately focus on flaws and shortcomings in the environment.

The typical solution for this problem is to choose a stylized world. A stylized world does not have to be cartoon oriented, but rather it can shoot for realism with a stylistic twist that gives the visuals their own coherent logic and consistency, based on color palette, recurring patterns, or details. Very often, designers take the natural aesthetics of low polygons, or of scattered polygon triangles arrangements, to build a design language that works within the limitations of the medium. An artificial world becomes believable, when it follows its own coherent design rules and principles (see Figure 3-11).

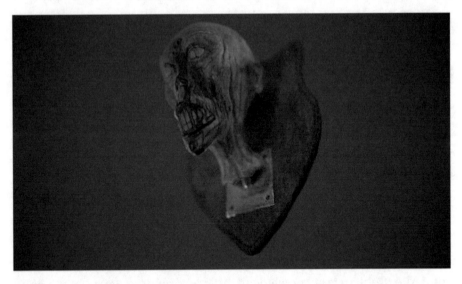

Figure 3-11. *Building stylized characters (image by C. Hillmann)*

Thinking vs. Overthinking VR

Developing a VR project is a dynamic process that should not get stuck at the concept stage. It is a good idea to go through fundamental question, to then move on to the practical side of generating actual results and building VR scenes that can be tested. The best approach is getting as quickly as possible to the point of testing ideas and iterating until something works. In the best-case scenario, a clear narrative that drives storytelling creates the visionary guidance to iterate and overcome production obstacles. Once the foundations are set, the GDD has evolved into a workable document, the art direction has been refined, and the technological hurdles have been mastered, it is time to tell a story.

Conclusion

In this chapter, we looked at some of the fundamental questions, starting with questioning the essence of what VR is, how it can be defined and how to determine if it is the right medium for our project. We discussed some of the most important ideas of how reality and perception are part of a centuries-old journey exploring the true nature of the human experience. We explored the ideas of reconstructing reality with clues, sensory input, and a cultural framework to understand what are the important driving forces that build our perception of a consistent and pleasant world experience.

To conceptualize and document an entire VR production with all contributions, components, concepts, visions and market expectations, we went over the core ingredients of a game design document and what it should entail. We continued by exploring how to best approach visual scripting by understanding the object-oriented nature of the Unreal Blueprint system.

Finally, we evaluated important design decisions, from audio, rotational navigation, to simulation sickness considerations to reflecting on the context-sensitive nature of the rules in VR (see Figure 3-12).

Figure 3-12. *VR development driven by vision (image by C. Hillmann)*

VR is still a wide field of experimentation, and the industry continues to refine and reinvent the best ways of reaching and containing consumers. The most practical approach is to focus on relevant storytelling, user testing, and iterations to find out what works best, using the documented experiences and recorded data from decades of research to piece together the elements that define a successful VR project.

In many ways, this is not just a technical or design question, but part of a grander vision of an emerging computational platform that is driven by imagination and cultural feedback, including values, beliefs, attitudes and memories, and the creativity of its visionaries, supported by the relentless enthusiasm and commitment of the VR communities that make it possible to merge art and science in an inspirational way.

CHAPTER 4

Unreal for VR: Basic Ingredients for an Oculus Go Project Setup

In this chapter, we look at the core concepts of creating a VR experience using the Unreal Engine. We'll take a quick look at how VR components are used across platforms, and then go straight into setting up an Oculus Go project right from the beginning. We will start with the prerequisites and initial setup followed by creating a project for testing different locomotion, teleportation, and object interaction concepts. After that we are going to build our scene using a pawn Blueprint with its components and event graphs, a level Blueprint for object interaction, and various material Blueprints to complete the scene. The basic concepts in this chapter are valid across all VR platforms and focus on the most common use cases for VR experiences.

© Cornel Hillmann 2019
C. Hillmann, *Unreal for Mobile and Standalone VR*,
https://doi.org/10.1007/978-1-4842-4360-2_4

High-End VR vs. Mobile and Standalone VR in Unreal

Unreal comes integrated with the Oculus VR, Google VR, Steam VR, OSVR, "right out of the box". This means the Unreal development environment covers the most important VR platforms with a unified toolset that uses consistent procedures for interaction components.

For VR development, we focus on the areas that are most important, which are locomotion and controller interaction. In principle, locomotion and controller setups are very similar between platforms. The biggest difference between high-end VR and mobile VR platforms is 6DOF vs. 3DOF, which has to be considered for interaction concepts (for example reaching out to grab an item with positional movement is only possible with a 6DOF motion controller). The biggest differentiators for mobile VR are the performance limitations, including the required techniques to work around the graphic limitations on the Android platform.

The Cross-Platform Advantage

The advantage of Unreal is that the development environment is consistent between platforms. A pawn camera component is automatically also a VR camera if VR is enabled, whether it is Oculus VR or Steam VR. The same goes for controllers. In Unreal, we have a Motion Controller (R) for the right hand and a Motion Controller (L) for the left hand. The controller device is consistent between devices. Setting up the motion controller for the Oculus Go, we will use the right Motion Controller (R) during development. If a user is left handed, the options to change the preferences are provided in the device setting (the setup for handedness using the motion source node, is covered in Chapter 5).

All we need to do is enable the Oculus VR plugin, install CodeWorks for Android, configure the project settings, the VR pawn and game mode, and start building our interaction components by using the Unreal Blueprint visual scripting system. In the following section, we will go through the setup steps to get our Unreal project up and running on the Oculus Go and then look at options for locomotion and controller interaction that are appropriate for our kind of VR project. These building blocks can easily be modified and transferred to any other platform using similar interaction mechanics.

Oculus Go Prerequisites

To deploy to Android, we need to install CodeWorks for Android by NVIDIA. The installer is included in the Unreal files in the Extras folder, inside the Engine folder. We will follow the default installation provided by Epic Games. CodeWorks for Android comes with the Android SDK, drivers, and platform tools to pack and deploy APK files for Android that we can use on the Oculus Go. Once the process is fired off from inside the Unreal editor, it is fully automated and there is no need to touch any of the CodeWorks for Android settings. The only directory inside the NVPACK installation folder that we will use is the Platform Tools directory, which contains the Android Debug Bridge (adb) application.

Basic Setup

Let's go through the basic steps to enable development on the Oculus Go.

1. Install CodeWorks for Android from the Unreal extras folder in the intended engine version (in this case Unreal 4.19) with the default locations as seen in Figure 4-1. The installer is preconfigured for Unreal (C:\Program Files\Epic Games\UE_4.19\ Engine\Extras\AndroidWorks\Win64). We will use the default settings. If prompted for NSight Tegra during the installation process, we choose Unselect and continue.

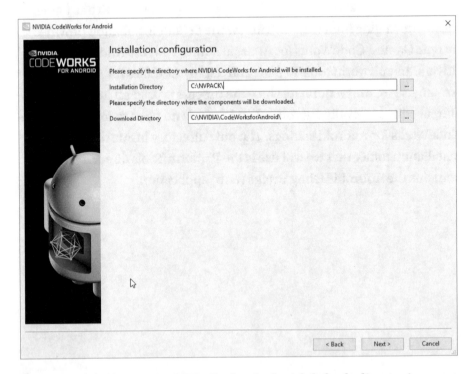

Figure 4-1. *NVIDIA CodeWorks for Android default directories*

2. Connect the Oculus Go and PC via USB and accept
    the terms and conditions from inside the headset.

3. Set up a developer account and an organization
    at `https://developer.oculus.com` to activate
    Developer mode (see Figure 4-2).

Figure 4-2. *Once the Oculus developer account is established, an
organization needs to be created to access developer features*

4. Enable developer mode with the Oculus Go companion
    app on our mobile phone under More Settings.

5. Open the C:\NVPACK\android-sdk-windows\
    platform-tools folder and Shift-click inside to launch
    PowerShell from the pop-up menu.

6. Using PowerShell, input **adb devices** and hit Enter.

7. After the security confirmation from inside the
    headset and repeating the **adb devices** input
    followed by Enter, our device ID is listed. In our
    case, it ends with the digits 8115 (see Figure 4-3).

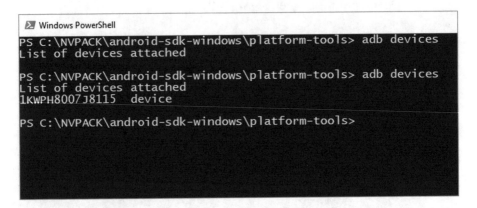

Figure 4-3. adb listing connected device

8. From the Epic Games Launcher, start a new Unreal
    project with the settings, Mobile/Tablet, Scalable 3D
    or 2D and No Starter Content (see Figure 4-4).

Figure 4-4. *New project settings without starter content*

9. From the main menu, under Edit ➤ Plugins, we will now verify that the Oculus VR plugin is the only VR plugin that is enabled in the Virtual Reality section of the Plugin page (see Figure 4-5) .

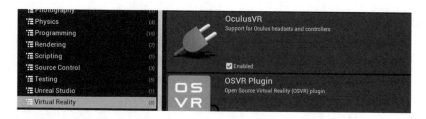

Figure 4-5. *The Oculus VR plugin is the only enabled plugin for the VR section*

10. Save the project and call the map Start.

11. Under the Edit ➤ Project Settings page, in the Maps
     & Modes section, we select our map called Start as
     the Editor Startup Map and the Game Default Map
     (see Figure 4-6).

Figure 4-6. *Setting the default map for the Unreal project*

12. Under the Edit ➤ Project Settings page, in the Input
     section, we disable the default Touch Interface
     setting to None by selecting Clear from the pop-up
     window (see Figure 4-7) .

Figure 4-7. *Disabling the touch interface*

13. From the Project Settings page, in the Platforms ➤
     Android section, we hit the Configure Now button
     inside of the red bar. It should turn green and
     display *Platform files are writable*. Under Minimum
     SDK and Target SDK, enter **19** (see Figure 4-8).

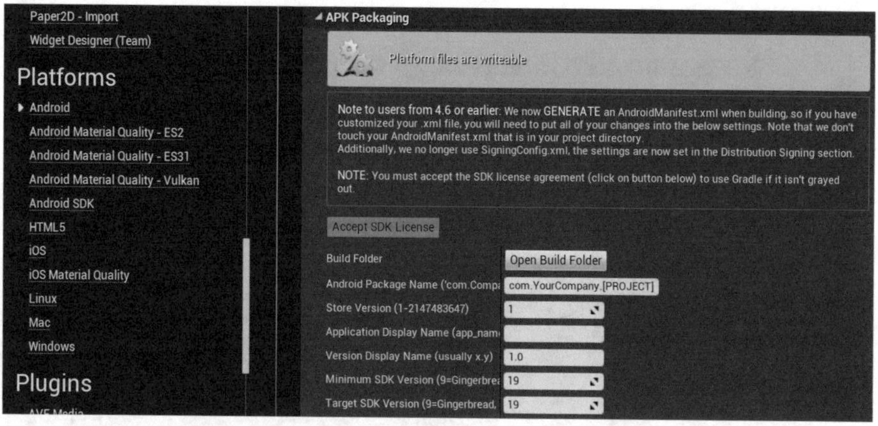

Figure 4-8. *The Android project settings*

14. On the Android page, enable configure the Android manifest for deployment to Gear VR (in later version referred to as Oculus Mobile instead of Gear VR) and enable full Screen immersive on KitKat and above devices, as seen in Figure 4-9.

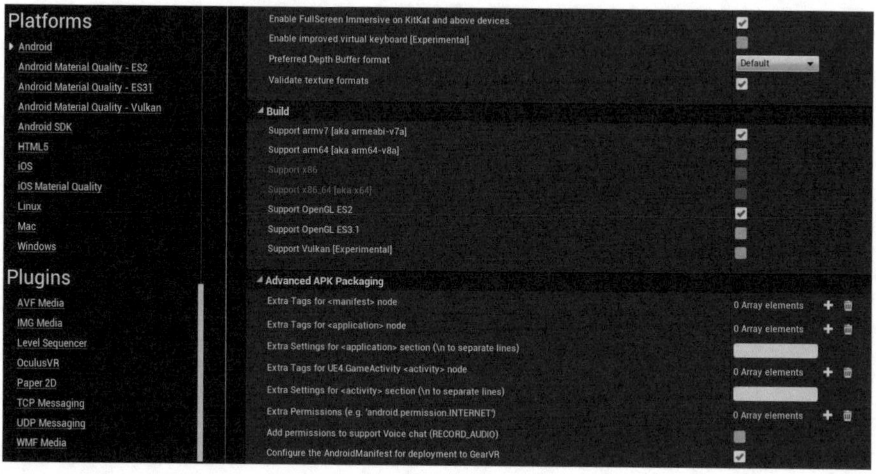

Figure 4-9. *The Gear VR / Oculus Mobile APK setting*

15. To deploy, go to File ➤ Package Project ➤ Android
     ➤ Android ASTC and package the project (see
     Figure 4-10) into a folder of your choice. The
     resulting APK file can then be sideloaded on the
     device.

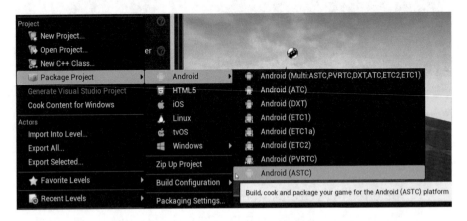

Figure 4-10. *The project is build and packaged for the Android*
platform

16. After the initial deployment of our new project
     to a local file, you can now deploy directly to the
     connected Oculus Go from the Launch menu. Once
     the device is connected using adb; it is listed under
     available devices from the launch pull-down menu
     (see Figure 4-11).

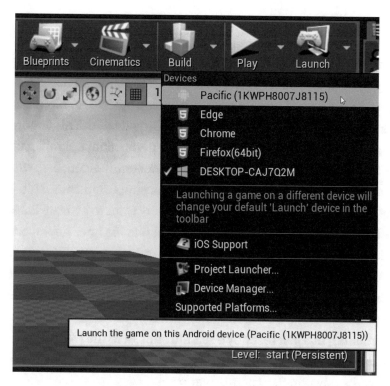

Figure 4-11. *Launching the Unreal project directly on the connected Oculus Go*

Once the project is initially launched on the Oculus Go, we have the option to test our projects in increments by saving after each change in the scene file, to review it inside of the headset. This allows us to quickly verify settings and functions while building our project.

Additional Project Settings

There are a number of additional settings on the Project Settings page that we may want to keep an eye on. First, in the Rendering section, Mobile HDR should be turned off; it is usually disabled by default. Mobile Multi-View and Mobile Multi-View Direct should be activated. This feature helps ease the CPU load and increases the overall performance significantly (there are only few situations where it is not recommended; e.g., when using dynamic shadows because they are not supported with Multi-View). On the Projects Settings Android page, we may want to activate Package Game Data Inside APK to keep everything in one file once deployed.

When it comes to OpenGL ES3.1 in the Android section, it should be noted that the current version on ES3.1 is not as optimized as the default ES2 version. ES3.1 comes with an improved shading model and should be the preferred choice, once fully supported by the engine. Vulkan (Experimental) has just recently been introduced to the Oculus Go and a lot of developers are looking forward to the final version of Vulkan, which will unify the development across platforms.

Fixed foveated rendering (FFR) is an option that is supported by the Oculus Go, it allows you to bring a higher resolution to the center of the lens, while rendering lower resolution tiles at the edges of the field of view where they are less noticed. To enable FFR, add a Set Tiled Multires Level node to the project, for example following an Event Begin Play node and select any of the three FFR levels (LMSLow, LMSMedium, or LMSHigh).

Doing a Packaging Test

At this point, without having done anything else other than setting up the VR options, the default pawn's camera is automatically linked to the active HMD and auto-activates. In the next step, we run a packaging test to get a functioning VR scene that allows us to look around. This allows us to validate that all required components work correctly, before we look into the different concepts for VR locomotion and motion controller interaction.

Inside the editor, we pull a cube from the Geometry tab on the left-hand menu and place it into the scene facing the player start icon for orientation purposes. We should now save the scene, if we haven't done it already, and will call this map Start. We will do a test build by going to the File menu and selecting Package Project ➤ Android ➤ Android (ASTC), as shown in Figure 4-10. Once we have selected a destination folder, the build process is initiated, and after a short while, we should see an APK file in that folder that we can install on the Oculus Go using adb commands.

Sideloading with adb

To get our APK file on the Oculus Go, we install it with the generated bat file, or move it into the adb directory, which is C:\NVPACK\android-sdk-windows\platform-tools. We Shift-right-click into the folder to launch Windows PowerShell. Type **install <name-of-app.apk>** and hit Enter. Once we select the app inside the Oculus Go under the Unknown Sources section in the library, we should launch into the minimal Unreal scene that we set up, a platform with a cube and a sky backdrop.

Having launched the file on the Oculus Go, it should allow us to look around. We have just uploaded a quick Unreal graphics test to the Oculus Go using sideloading with adb. Two other useful adb commands should be noted. To have all apps installed on the Go listed, type **adb shell pm list packages** and hit Enter. To uninstall an app from that list, enter **adb uninstall <packagename>** and hit Enter. Sideloading is not only a way of bypassing the Oculus Go store and installing apps directly on the headset, it is also very often used for limited distribution B2B apps, or for installing specialized software that that is not available in the official Oculus store.

Launching Directly on Oculus Go

After having packed the initial project to a local folder, we are now ready to launch it directly on the Oculus Go. To do that, we must have an active adb connection with a recognized device, as we set it up earlier.

If we go to the launch icon in the top-row menu bar, we should be able to select our Android device from the pull-down menu by its adb device ID. Once we select the Oculus Go as a launch device, Unreal will build the project directly on the device. After we get the success message from our output log under Window ➤ Developer Tools ➤ Output Log, we can put on the headset and view the current scene. In the next step we will do a proper setup that includes a VR game mode, a VR pawn, a motion controller component and a basic locomotion setup.

VR Game Mode, Pawn, and Input Setup

To create a VR game mode, we right-click into the content browser, select Blueprint class, then Game Mode Base from the pop-up menu, and name it VR_Gamemode (see Figure 4-12). A game mode contains the basic rules for a game or experience and defines what the default pawn is and what pawn the player spawns from when entering the game. Very often, the game mode is also used for information that is stored between maps.

Next, we create the VR pawn. We set it up by right-clicking the content browser and selecting Blueprint class from the pop-up window (see Figure 4-12).

Figure 4-12. *Blueprint parent classes*

From the options of the Parent Class menu, we select Pawn and name it VR_Pawn. We will now set the VR game mode and the VR pawn as our defaults by selecting VR Game mode in the Game Mode Override in World Settings window and in the Project Settings section Maps & Modes from the pull-down menu. Opening our VR game mode, we will set our VR pawn as the default and save (see Figure 4-13).

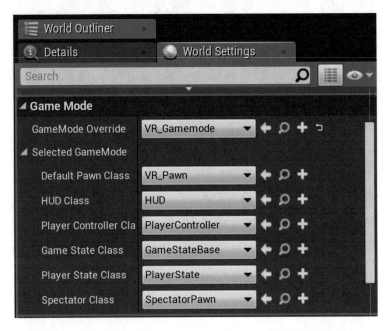

Figure 4-13. *The currently selected VR_gamemode in the GameMode Override in World Settings*

In the Details panel, having our VR pawn selected, we set Auto Possess to Player 0 (see Figure 4-14).

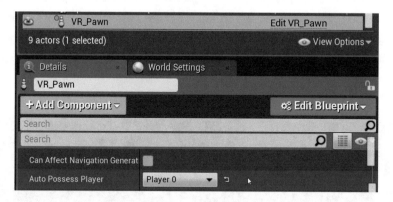

Figure 4-14.   *Setting Auto Posses Player 0 for the VR Pawn*

This guarantees that we are automatically assigned to use the VR pawn as our default player.

Next, we will set the input bindings in the Input section of the project settings. Under Action Mappings, we click the plus icon twice and assign Motion Controller (R) Thumbstick Right to Snap Rotate Right and Motion Controller (R) Thumbstick Left to Snap Rotate Left. Under Axis Mappings, we add one entry by clicking the plus icon and assign Motion Controller (R) Trigger to Movement, with a scaling factor of 0.3 to slow it down (see Figure 4-15).

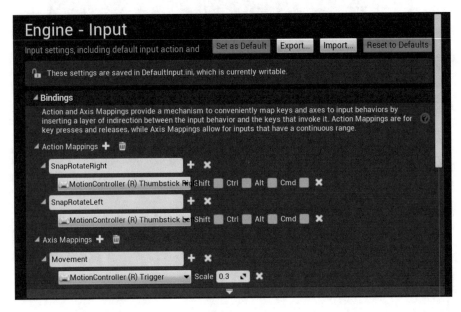

Figure 4-15. *Setting the input bindings*

Setting up VR Pawn Components

Next, we will set up our VR Pawn by double-clicking and opening the VR pawn's Blueprint viewport. The components help us set up the motion controller functions, such as the laser beam and reticle, and to control the movement for our VR Pawn. From the Add Component menu, we add a scene component and rename it Camera Root. Next, we add a camera component, plus another scene component and rename it Controller Root. Following that, we add a motion controller component, a static mesh component that we rename Controller Mesh, a particle system component that we rename Laser Beam, a cylinder component that we rename Cylinder Reticle and a floating pawn movement component. We should now have a total of 9 components under the VR_Pawn components tab.

We rearrange the components in a way that the camera and the controller root are parented to the camera root, the motion controller is parented to the controller root, the controller mesh is parented to the motion controller and the laser beam and cylinder reticle are parented to the controller mesh, as seen in Figure 4-16.

Figure 4-16. *Component hierarchy for the VR Pawn*

In this setup, the camera root and the controller root are dummy components that allow us to offset the positioning value in the event graph. The Floating Pawn Movement component is not a screen component; therefore, it does not need to be parented. It provides very basic directional movement for the pawn. The *controller mesh* that is parented to the *motion controller* allows us to use the Oculus Go 3D model that is part of the Oculus VR plugin content. Without this extra static mesh component, the motion controller's setting would only allow to display the Gear VR mesh under the motion controller's visualization section. In the Details panel, from the Static Mesh section, we select the Oculus Go Controller Mesh, and in the Materials tab, the Oculus Go Controller Material (see Figure 4-17).

Figure 4-17. *Assigning 3D mesh and material to the controller mesh*

All components need to be zeroed out in their location settings, so they sit at the center. We will now resize cylinder reticle to the scale settings of X = 0.05, Y = 0.05, Y = 0.002, and under the Rendering section in the Details panel, we uncheck Visible. This ensures the reticle is initially not visible.

Setting up Event Graph Blueprints for the VR Pawn

To move, rotate our view, and use the controller to interact, we will set up our basic Blueprints (see Figure 4-18).

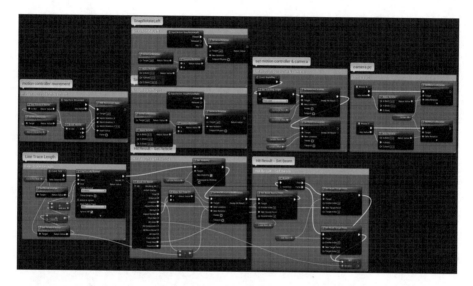

Figure 4-18. *The VR Pawn's event graph with eight basic Blueprint sections*

The Blueprints are Motion Controller Movement, Snap Rotate Right, Snap Rotate Left, Set Motion Controller & Camera, Laser & Reticle, and Camera PC. Camera PC is basically just a temporary helper Blueprint, which allows us to control the camera at runtime on the PC to inspect scene items. We will go through each individual Blueprint and set it up. To test our VR pawn, we drop it into the level.

Simple Motion Controller Locomotion

We want to continually move in the direction the motion controller is pointing at by pressing the trigger button, while staying on the floor. In the VR pawn's event graph, we search with the right-click menu for the Movement nodes and connect them as seen in Figure 4-19.

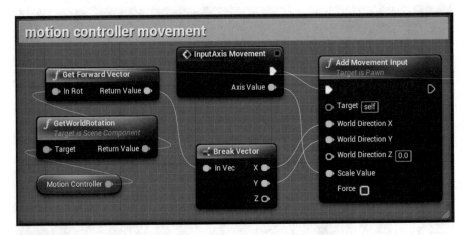

Figure 4-19. *The motion controller movement Blueprint*

The Blueprint is fired off with the Movement input event that we defined earlier in the input bindings. It drives the Add Movement Input node, which gets its direction from the motion controllers' forward vector. To make sure we stay on the floor, we break the forward vector and only use the X and Y direction.

Snap Rotation

Next, we want to rotate the direction of our VR pawns in 30-degree increments to quickly turn around. For this movement, we will use the two other input bindings we set up earlier, which are Snap Rotate Right and Snap Rotate Left. These input events are used to fire off the Set Actor Rotation node as seen in Figure 4-20.

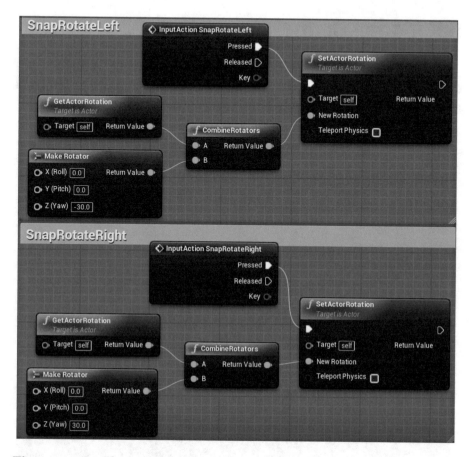

Figure 4-20. *The snap rotation Blueprints*

To rotate our pawn, we simply combine our actors' rotation with a make rotator node that is set to 30 degrees for the right rotation and minus 30 degrees for the left rotation. Once the event is fired off, each click on the left or right side of the touchpads will rotate the view, respectively.

Set Motion Controller

To set the pawn's height and motion controller, we need to set up its tracking origin and relative offset using the controller root and camera root components (see Figure 4-21).

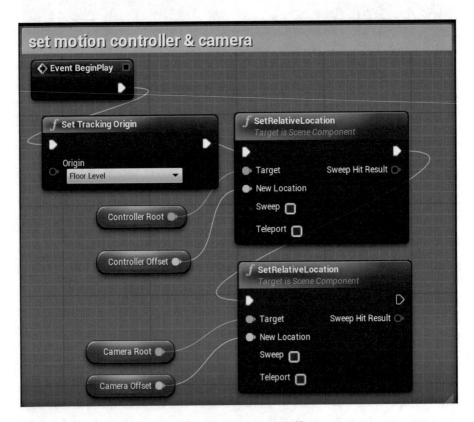

Figure 4-21. *Initializing the motion controller*

Event Begin Play sets the tracking origin of motion controllers at the floor level and is then adjusted to a relative position, which is set by the Z value of the vector variable that we set up with the name Camera Offset (see Figure 4-22). By adjusting the Z value, we can easily go in and adjust the initial height at any time.

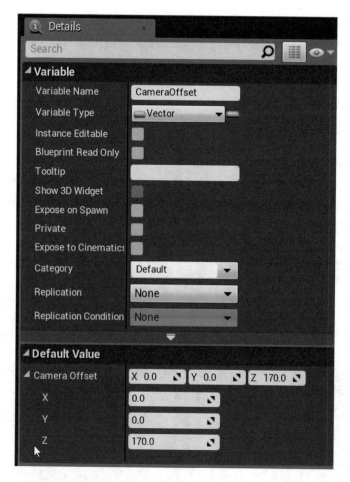

Figure 4-22. *Setting up a Vector variable for the Z axis according to the pawn's height*

For the controller root offset we follow the same procedure. We create a vector variable and connect it to the Set Relative Location node. At this point we will leave the controller offset unchanged with a 0 offset value on the X, Y and Z axis. The motion controller positions itself automatically to the default position in relation to the camera. Having an Controller Offset vector variable available in our default setup allows us to tweak the controller offset position at any time. Tweaking the controller offset becomes important when adjusting the position for guns, or other in-game controller replacement meshes.

PC Camera Setup

To be able to look around in our scene at runtime on the PC, we will set up camera controls. These are just temporary auxiliary helper controls to inspect screen items. We can delete this Blueprint once the project is finished (see Figure 4-23).

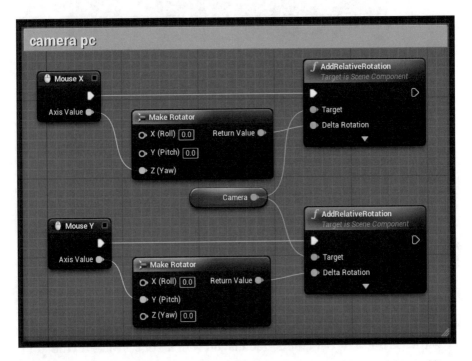

Figure 4-23. *PC camera setup*

We drag the camera from the VR pawn's components and connect it to an Add Relative Rotation node, driven by mouse X and mouse Y axes input events, which are connected to a Make Rotator node for *yaw (Mouse X)* and *pitch (Mouse Y)* movements.

Laser Beam and Reticle Setup

Typically, the directional visualization of the VR motion controller borrows its appearance from a laser pointer, such as a red glowing forward beam. To set this up as a system, we need to track a start point and an end point for a laser beam particle system with its material settings. Once the laser beam hits an object, we want to see a reticle in the form of a red dot that floats on the hit object. In addition to that, we want to store the information of what object was hit in a variable, so that we can pass this information on and use it in our level Blueprint to interact with the hit item. This Blueprint's centerpiece is the Line Trace By Channel node. The channel we are referring to is the visibility of scene objects. Figure 4-24 shows an overview of the Blueprint.

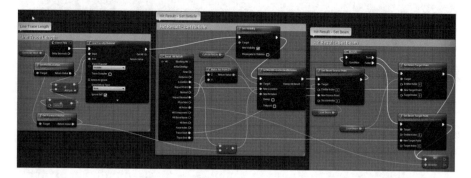

Figure 4-24. *Line trace, reticle, and laser beam setup overview*

We will look at this Blueprint in two parts. First, the information that we feed into the Line Trace By Channel node. Second, the data that we can pull out of the hit information and use for our reticle, beam, and object interaction in two sections.

113

In Figure 4-25, we see that the node is driven by an even tick and the controller mesh world location is provided as a starting point. The forward vector with one UE unit, which equals one centimeter, is multiplied by 5,000 and added to the world location to provide the end point of the ray-tracing operation.

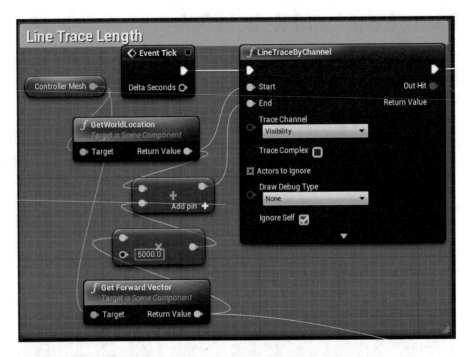

Figure 4-25. *The input of the line trace by channel node*

On the output of the Line Trace By Channel node (see Figure 4-26), we will break the hit result into the individual pins that we get, by using the break hit result node. The event tick is first piped into a set visibility node for the cylinder reticle, to enable its visibility, as it was initially set to off by default. The next node, Set World Rotation And Location, places the reticle as floating spot above the hit surface, by getting the impact normal vector. From here, all we need are the two axes that we feed into the new rotation value.

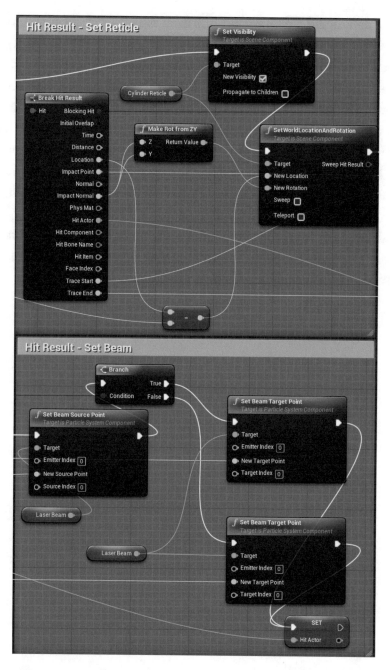

Figure 4-26. *Hit result for cylinder reticle and laser beam, from left to right*

The new location data we can pull from the hit result location pin. To have the reticle float slightly above the surface, for better visibility, we subtract the original vector from the input. The following nodes in the tick chain set the beginning and the end of the laser beam component on our VR pawn. The laser beam starts at the break hit result, trace start point. We check with a branch node, if we receive a blocking hit from the line trace. If this is true, this means the laser beam will end at the hit result impact point. If this is false, the beam target point is set at its full length, which is the trace end from the break hit result. To actually see the laser beam, we will set up the particle generator and material for it.

The last node is an object reference variable that we create and call hit actor. This pulls the object information from the scene and lets us reference it in the level Blueprint for further object interaction.

Setting up Particles and Material for the Laser Beam

To give the beam material a glowing appearance, we need a translucent, emissive material with a transparent fall-off. To do that we create a new material by right-clicking into the content browser and selecting material from the Create Basic Asset section of the menu. In the Material setting, we set the blend mode to Translucent. From the Palette window, we select a Text Coord node. We pull the fall-off from the Text Coord node by masking one channel (g). The Multiply, Sine, and Power nodes are placed to emphasize the result, which is multiplied with the color and alpha channel of the particle color expression (see Figure 4-27).

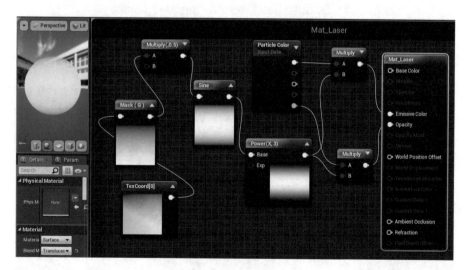

Figure 4-27. *The beam material setup*

To create a particle system, we right-click the content browser and select Particle System from Basic Assets. Inside the Particle editor (see Figure 4-28), we right-click the emitter and create the following modules and settings under the Details panel.

- Type data > Beam data. Details: Beam method - target, speed: 0

- Beam > Source. Details: Source method - user set

- Beam > Target. Details: Source method - user set

- Color > Initial color. Details: Start color > distribution > constant RGB = 1,0,0

From the existing modules, we change the following settings.

- Required > Details: Set material - set mat_laser (material from Figure 4-27)

- Initial Size > Details: Start size, max, min - set all to 0.5

Figure 4-28. *The required section of the particle beam*

Finally, we remove the Color Over Life module by deleting it.

We can leave the other modules, Initial Velocity and Lifetime, at their default values.

Having set up the beam particle system and the material, we can now go back into the VR pawn event graph, select the particle system component, and add the particle system into the particles slot on the details panel.

Creating Interactions in the Level Blueprint

After completing our VR pawn with functioning laser beam emitted from the motion controller and a reticle on surfaces where the beam hits, we are now ready to design our first scene interaction. The most basic interaction with an object is a highlight when the item is selected, similar to hovering over a button on a webpage. To swap a color for a highlight color on our cube that we placed into the scene earlier, we need to create a material instance.

A material instance is a performance-efficient way to change a material by exposed parameters. First, we create our master material by right-clicking and setting up a standard material with a color input node. To access the color input in the instanced version of the material, we right-click the Color node and select Convert To Parameter, as seen in Figure 4-29.

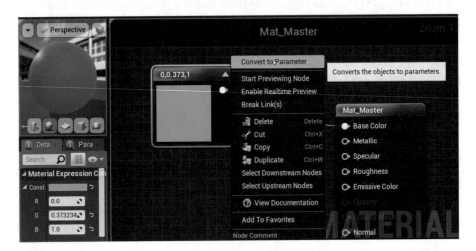

Figure 4-29. *Converting the color node to a parameter*

We can now select the original material in the asset browser, right-click and select Create Material Instance. After naming the instance, we can open the material instance and edit the color parameter that we set. We change it to a lighter blue variation to indicate it is highlighted and selected (see Figure 4-30).

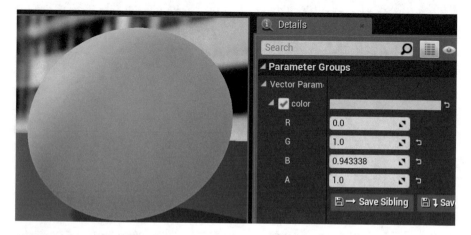

Figure 4-30. *Editing the exposed color parameter for the material instance*

Now we have the two material states for our cube: unselected (darker blue), selected (lighter blue). We assign the un-selected blue to our cube and open the level Blueprint. Up to this point, we have set up all interaction in the VR pawns event graph. Now that we are dealing with a separate object in the scene, the cube (in our case, called Newcube), we need to communicate between the VR pawn and the cube in order to interact. In this case, we will use the level Blueprint and the object variable, *hit actor*, to pull the information that we need from the VR pawn (see Figure 4-31). We can access the level Blueprint from the top toolbar under the Blueprints icon: Blueprints ➤ Level Blueprints ➤ Open Level Blueprint.

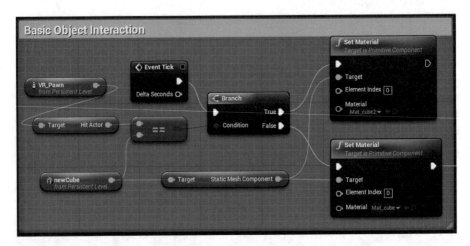

Figure 4-31. *The level Blueprint interaction between pawn and cube*

When the hit actor variable of our VR pawn is equal to the cube in the scene named Newcube, we will fire off a branch that is driven by an event tick. If the stated condition is true, the cube will have its material set to the lighter-blue material instance; if is not true, the material is set to its original darker-blue material.

We have added basic interaction with a scene object, in addition to the smooth locomotion, snap rotation, motion controller beam and reticle functions of our VR pawn.

In the next section, we change the smooth locomotion to a more commonly used teleportation movement using fixed teleportation destinations.

Setting up Fixed Teleportation Destinations

Fixed teleportation locations are very often used in presentation apps or educational VR titles. They allow control of where the user experiences the scene, and they are often used in mobile and standalone VR titles because they allow a great degree of control over the user experience, while managing scene resources and performance.

In the following setup, we will get rid of the previous smooth locomotion, replace it with a teleportation mechanic, and add trigger events to our motion controller. Before getting into the Blueprint layout, we need to arrange and set up the graphic assets for the teleportation destinations.

Each teleportation destination has three parts: (a) the floor object, which is a translucent, slowly evolving circular object on the floor that is visible at all times and indicates that this is a valid teleportation destination; (b) a cylinder target mesh that is invisible, but takes the hits from the laser beam; and (c) a billboard sprite Blueprint with a 2D image that is always facing the camera and only visible when the cylinder is hit. Figure 4-32 shows the two floor objects and the billboard sprites for the hit visualization, temporarily made visible, while each cylinder for the hit action is set to invisible.

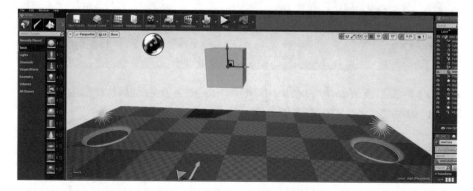

Figure 4-32. *The two teleportation destinations*

The material for the floor object is slowly evolving with an upward movement, the material parameters (see Figure 4-33) blends an irregular striped texture moving slowly upward through a Panner node with a bright blue in a linear additive blend node for the emissive color, while the opacity channel is fed with a modified gradient to taper off and fade out the material into 100% transparent. The up-facing side of the material is masked out with the help of a Pixel Normal WS expression. Because we are using an upside-down cone, we don't want the flat surface to be visible. The overall opacity is limited with a Clamp node at maximum 0.3.

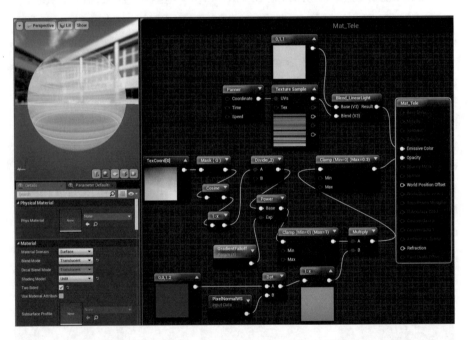

Figure 4-33. *A slowly evolving translucent material that fades into transparency and masked out up-facing side*

If we don't have an irregular striped texture at hand, we can create one quickly in Photoshop by slicing any image that has a good amount of variety with a vertical cut that is one pixel wide. Once we have a slice that is one pixel wide, we expand the image size horizontally by the same pixel amount as the height. We can now colorize this new striped image, so the color range is roughly within the same hue range.

Level Blueprint for Trigger Action and Teleportation

We will expand the previous Blueprint for object interaction from Figure 4-31, to include trigger action and teleportation. In Figure 4-34, we see an overview, which includes Object Interaction, Teleport Sprite Visualization, Activate New Level, and Teleportation. We will look at each section individually.

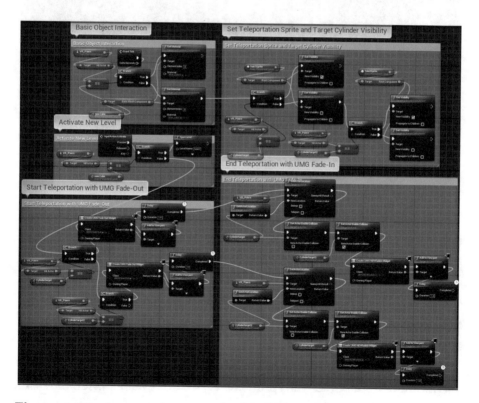

Figure 4-34. *An overview over the level Blueprints*

We will expand the previous object interaction from Figure 4-31, starting with the False branch output from set material. In this context that basically means, if we are not pointing at the cube, we will continue to evaluate what else we might be pointing at. To do that we pipe the event tick into a branch where the True branch sets the visibility on and the False output sets the visibility off (see Figure 4-35).

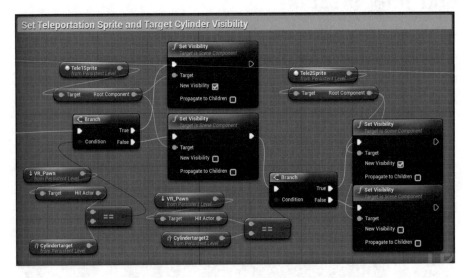

Figure 4-35. *The teleportation target sprite hit visualization*

The condition is that the hit actor from the VR pawn is equal to the respective target, in this case Cylinder Target and Cylinder Target 2. The Hit Actor variable is the output from the VR pawn line trace that we set up earlier, it checks if our VR pawn's controller beam is hitting the invisible cylinder by checking if hit actor and Cylinder Target are equal. If that is true, the visibility of the target sprite is activated; if false, the visibility is deactivated.

If we point our controller's beam into the direction above the teleportation floor object, the sprite object becomes visible when the beam hits the invisible cylinder.

Building the Trigger Action

To use the motion controller trigger for object interaction, we delete the previous movement input mapping in the project settings Input Bindings section. Here we add a new action mapping named Activate, and select the Motion Controller (R) trigger as the connected input.

We can now right-click and bring up Input Action Activate into the level Blueprint. We drag off the pressed pin and connect it to a branch, where we define the condition, that if our VR pawn's motion controller hits the object named Newcube, we get a branch result. If the condition is true, we'll send it to Open Level node, which will open a new map that we call tele 2 (see Figure 4-36). In the content browser, we create a new empty map with the same name by right-clicking and selecting Create New Level.

Figure 4-36. *Activating a new level with the motion controller trigger button*

Setting up Fade-out and Fade-in for Teleportation

From the trigger action's false branch, we continue to build our teleportation targets as trigger targets. But before we can do that, we need to build two components that allow us to fade-out and fade-in again. Fading has been established as good practice when using teleportation, as it allows the user to ease in and out of the current location. Normally, this would be done with an Unreal sequencer fade track. However, the problem is that sequencer fade tracks don't work on mobile platforms as they require post-processes with mobile HDR, which has to be turned off for mobile VR for performance reasons at this point. The alternative is to create one UMG widget for fade out and one UMG widget to fade back in and trigger them in our level Blueprint.

To create a UMG widget, we right-click into the content browser and select widget Blueprint from the use interface menu. Opening the widget, we find the UMG Widget Designer section, which allows us to create user interface elements on a layered canvas.

In the Details section of the Canvas panel, we set Render Transform ➤ Transform ➤ Scale to 2.5 for X and 2.5 for Y. We add an image from the Palette selection, and set the appearance under Color and Opacity to Black.

Under Details ➤ Slot ➤ Anchors, we set the size X to 1920 and size Y to 1080. We set the slot anchors maximum settings for X and Y to 1.0. We are now ready to create the fade effect. From the Animations tab, we create an animation track for the opacity over one second (see Figure 4-37).

Figure 4-37. *Creating a fade track in the UMG widget designer section*

Once the track has been created in the Designer section, it becomes available as an animation component in the Graph section of the widget Blueprint. In the Graph section (see Figure 4-38), we will place a Play Animation node that is driven by an even construct and has our Fade Out track as the targeted animation. We connect the output pin to a one-second delay, before the Remove From Parent node is connected. The delay is needed because the animation lasts one second and the output of the Play Animation node triggers immediately. The Remove From Parent node is needed to remove the fade animation from our viewport after completion.

Figure 4-38.   *The event graph for the fade animation widget*

We will create a second widget for a fade-in by copying the UMG widget in the content browser, renaming it, and reversing the opacity animation.

Setting up the Teleportation Blueprint

We continue with the false output from the previous trigger action in Figure 4-36 and input it into a new branch with the condition that our VR pawn's motion controller beam is hitting the invisible cylinder of the first teleportation target. The cylinder is invisible, but has collision enabled, so it is taking hits. In Figure 4-39, we see an overview over both sections of the teleportation Blueprint.

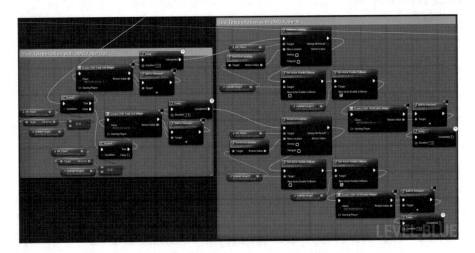

Figure 4-39. *The teleportation Blueprint overview (1/3)*

If it is true that the cylinder is hit, we will execute a UMG fade-out widget. We right-click, select Create Widget, insert the UMG fadeout widget into the Class slot, and insert the node after the true branch. From the return value pin, we have to pull out a connection and search for Add To Viewport, connect it, and add a one-second delay, to make sure the animation has finished before the next action is triggered (see Figure 4-40).

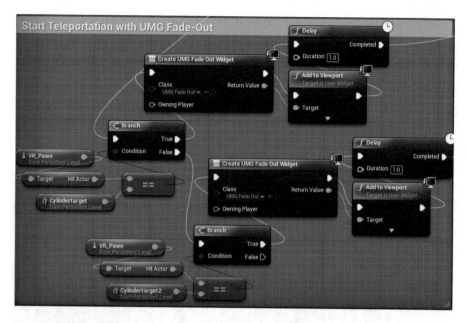

Figure 4-40.   *The teleportation Blueprint (2/3)*

Once the fade-out is completed, we get the actor location of the hit cylinder, which is our teleportation target and set our VR pawn to the new location In the last part of our teleportation Blueprint, we disable the collision for our teleportation target cylinder and enable it for all other teleportation targets. We do that to disable collision errors with our motion controller while sitting inside the invisible target cylinder.

After that, we create the fade-in UMG widget, add it to the viewport, and add a one-second delay, so that the animation can finish before the next action takes place (see Figure 4-41). The fade-in UMG is the last node in the chain, so the delay would actually not be needed, as there is no action after it. We leave in the chain anyway as a reminder, in case we plan to add anything.

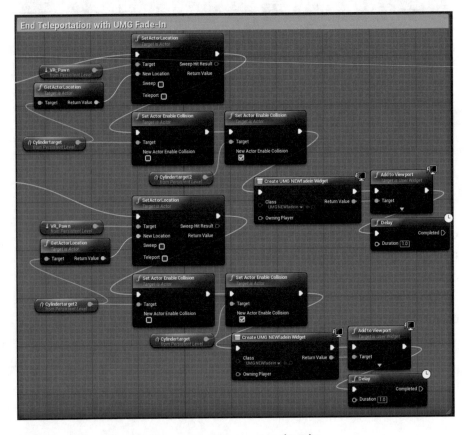

Figure 4-41. *The teleportation Blueprint (3/3)*

The teleportation Blueprint is now complete. If we test it on the Oculus Go, the target sprite shows when the invisible cylinder is hit. When we push the trigger, the headset fades to black before it fades from black to transparent at the new location.

Setting up a Fixed Target On-Rails Locomotion

Fixed target on-rail locomotion is very popular in mobile and standalone VR apps. This locomotion variation gives the user the sensation of moving through a 3D scene by selecting fixed targets, which triggers a movement from point A to point B. The movement replaces the fade-out, fade-in mechanic in our scene. To set it up in our scene, we delete the fade-related nodes and insert a Timeline and a Lerp Vector node (see Figure 4-42).

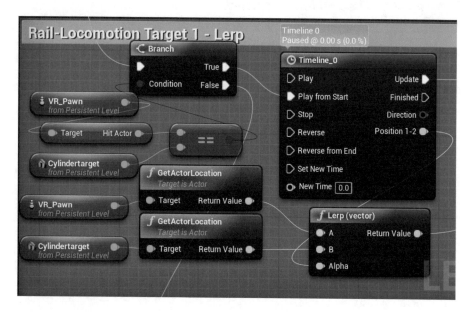

Figure 4-42. *The timeline and lerp vector nodes*

We open up the timeline and insert a float track with two keyframes: one at zero with value zero, and one at two with value one. We name the curve position 1-2. The timeline helps us to transition between two values, by plugging it into the Lerp Alpha input (see Figure 4-43). All we have to do now is connect the two inputs, one for the current position of our VR pawn, the other for the target position that we used for the teleportation mechanic.

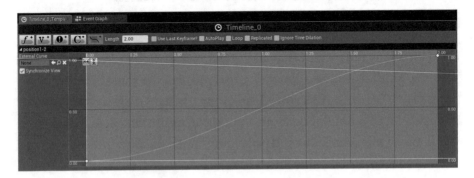

Figure 4-43. *The timeline float track*

We do the same procedure for the second target. Each lerp timeline movement should move our VR pawn into the desired position. The three ending nodes, Set Actor Position and Set Actor Enable Collision remain the same from the previous teleportation setup (see Figure 4-44).

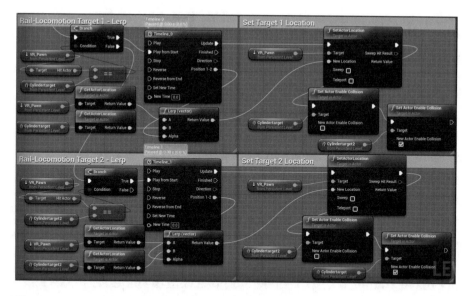

Figure 4-44. *The complete fixed target on-rails locomotion Blueprint*

Flexible Teleportation

Previously, we looked at fixed target teleportation and fixed target on-rails locomotion. We will now look at one of the most common teleportation styles that allow free exploration of a VR scene. The mechanic is somewhat similar to our laser pointer reticle, but without the beam and with a 2D sprite image instead of the cylinder reticle.

The objective is to create a Blueprint that detects if the motion controller line trace hits a floor, and if it does, positions a sprite image at the hit location. We then want the trigger to execute the teleportation without using the fade-out/fade-in widgets. This Blueprint will allow us to freely select any position on the ground as a teleportation target and instantly move to a position of our own choice, instead of a fixed position.

Expanding the VR Pawn's Blueprint with a Floor Reticle

To detect if we hit a floor surface with our VR pawn's motion controller laser beam, we need to expand the previous Line Trace By Channel Blueprint that was used for all surfaces and branch off the events for making the floor sprite reticle visible if a floor surface is detected. A floor surface is any surface where the surface normals face up. We create the floor reticle by placing a material with a 2D target image on a plane mesh item which we parent to the motion controller mesh, as we did with the surface hit reticle (Figure 8-8 in Chapter 8 shows the floor sprite image).

We will expand the Blueprint from Figure 4-24 and hook up the event tick that is coming out of the line trace node with the required nodes for floor detection and reticle as seen in Figure 4-44. In the following section, we are zooming in on the newly created part on the top left and then to the final part on the top right (see Figure 4-45).

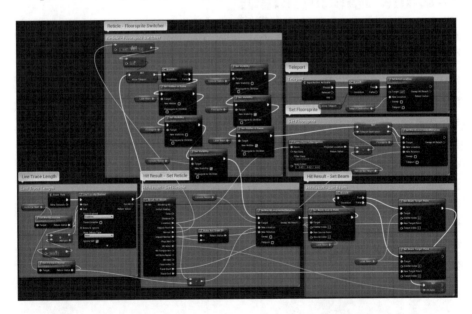

Figure 4-45. *Expanding the line trace by channel result with floor detection*

The outcoming yellow normal vector that we extract from the line trace by channel, we pipe through a dot product with Z = 1 and compare if it is greater than 0.9. If this is the case, we set a boolean variable named Allow Teleport. If Allow Teleport is *true*, we make the regular laser beam reticle invisible, make the floor-sprite visible, and then set the laser beam hidden in game (see Figure 4-46). Next, we add a Project Point To Navigation node, which limits the teleportation target positions to the navigation mesh that we will add later.

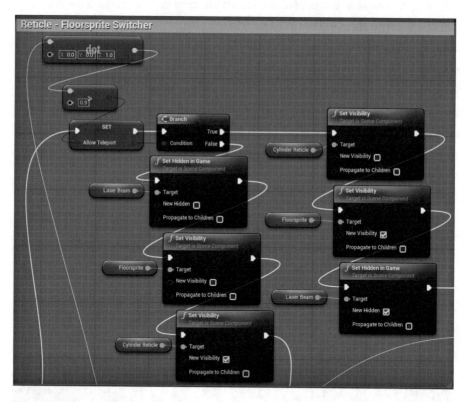

Figure 4-46. *Floor detection and floor sprite visibility*

The navigation mesh helps us to control the teleportation targets. It automatically detects collisions and creates spacing around collision areas to avoid clipping. Plus, it disables areas that are not reachable, such as spaces under furniture pieces, and so forth. From the resulting vector, we deduct a vector variable that we set freely, and this helps us to offset the location destination's height by value that we set in the variable's z-vector.

The *nav mesh* is usually slightly above the ground, and with the *reduce nav height* variable we can adjust the position. Next, we set a new vector variable *teleport destination* for reference and then insert the output into the Set World Location and Rotation node. We pull the rotation information from the same hit pin that was driving our regular surface laser beam reticle. The actual teleportation action is executed with the Activate input action. It checks with a branch if the location we are pointing at is an allowed teleportation destination by checking the variable condition that we set up in Figure 4-46. If teleportation is allowed, the teleportation destination variable is used for the new position (see Figure 4-47).

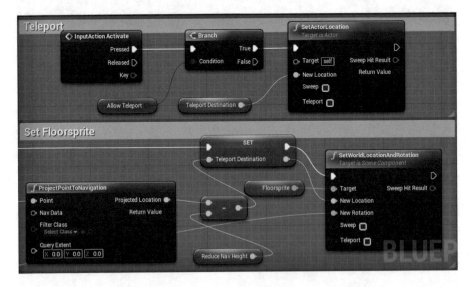

Figure 4-47. *Setting the floor-detection sprite*

To test our scene, we will add a stairs mesh and three cone meshes from the Geometry tab, plus a nav mesh bounds volume from the Volumes tab. The *nav mesh volume* should be large enough to cover all our geometry pieces, including the floor. Pressing the *p* shortcut allows us to review the nav mesh result, which is shown as a green surface floating above the ground. In this example, we are using the default settings of the nav mesh.

In case we want to tweak specific values, such as cell height and radius, we can change the settings in the Project Settings page under Engine ➤ Navigation Mesh. Once we deploy the result to our Oculus Go, we are able to use the flat surface areas of the stairs as teleportation targets and to teleport to all nav mesh areas, while areas that were excluded in the nav mesh, such as the space below the cones, are not available as teleportation targets. Our system automatically switches from floor detection with a floor target sprite, to a non-floor surface with laser beam and regular reticle when a non-floor surface is hit (see Figure 4-48).

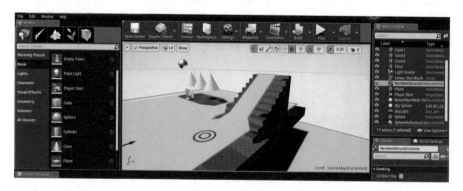

Figure 4-48. *NavMesh visualization (green) and floor sprite reticle (red)*

Conclusion

In this chapter, we went over the basic VR approaches in Unreal. We looked at the components that Unreal uses cross-platform for VR, such as the camera and motion controller. We then went through all the steps necessary to start an Oculus Go project. We set up the prerequisites and the initial connection with the device to do a graphics test.

Next, we implemented a test project using motion controller-based smooth locomotion, snap rotation, input bindings, and basic setups for a motion controller beam, reticle, and object interaction, including the needed material setup. In the next project variation, we investigated how to set up teleportation with teleportation targets and fade mechanics using UMG widgets. We looked at creating materials for teleportation targets, as well as how to use fixed targets for on-rails locomotion.

Finally, we set up a flexible teleportation system with floor detection to freely teleport between positions of our own choice. We looked at how to load a new level with the motion controller trigger button and how to implement a nav mesh volume at a target for our target position. This chapter covered the very basic ingredients for a VR experience on the Oculus Go.

CHAPTER 5

Comparing the Gear VR, Oculus Go, and Oculus Quest

Introduction

In this chapter, we look at the key differences between the Gear VR, the Oculus Go, and the Oculus Quest (based on prerelease information and subject to change when it ships). Even though each one of these headsets runs on an Android operating system, hardware differences play an important role when targeting the individual headset and its use. We will compare hardware specifications and different input events, and learn how to assign them in Unreal.

To manage handedness on the Gear VR and the Oculus Go motion controller, we will set up a Blueprint. Comparing the strength and weaknesses between the hardware options, we will look at how these headsets are being used in their markets and how they tie into the major market trends for consumers and businesses that will shape the future of the industry.

© Cornel Hillmann 2019
C. Hillmann, *Unreal for Mobile and Standalone VR*,
https://doi.org/10.1007/978-1-4842-4360-2_5

Technical Comparison

Let's look at how the technical specification of the Samsung and Oculus mobile and standalone HMD lineup compares and at the key differences in developing for it. The differences will give us an idea of what applications are best for each headset type and how consumers and businesses can take advantages of the options available.

The Gear VR

The Samsung Gear VR is a cooperation between Samsung and Oculus, in which Samsung provides the hardware and Oculus provides the software. The Gear VR is part of Samsung's lineup of wearable devices and supports its flagship smartphones, the Galaxy series, starting with the Galaxy S6. It comes with a 3DOF motion controller, which was introduced in March 2017 alongside the launch of the Galaxy S8 (see Figure 5-1).

Figure 5-1. *The Samsung Gear VR (photo by C. Hillmann)*

Smartphone-based, snap-in VR HMDs have advantages and disadvantages over standalone VR headsets. The biggest advantage is social media discovery. By tapping on the VR icon in 360 photos or videos on social media posts or web pages using the smartphone, the user is prompted to put on the headset in order to get a fully immersed view in VR (see Figure 5-2).

To open this application, insert your device into your Gear VR.

Figure 5-2. *Opening a social media VR post*

This feature allows you to tie in VR with other media types. For example, a tour guide could list tourist destinations with a VR link on each description page, providing the user with the opportunity to get an immersive view directly from the info page if desired. This direct connection between web pages and social media is an easy entry point for user discovery and has been successfully implemented for tourism, marketing, real estate, and education. It is also a good way to guide an audience with headsets to the right entry points by using specific web or social media pages as launch pads. For VR content developers, this feature is a good opportunity to create marketing content. For example, a game developer can post 360 snapshots of a title in development as a teaser for the game's environment art.

In Chapter 2, we discussed how to capture an Unreal scene using the stereo panoramic movie plugin. The captured images can be used for a Facebook 360 post by injecting Facebook metadata or by using one of the Photoshop templates that Facebook provides. The template includes the required metadata to make the image work as an active launchable 360 experience (see facebook360.fb.com/editing-360-photos-injecting-metadata).

One other advantage of the Gear VR is the fact that it can use the smartphone's camera in VR. Even though this feature has not been used much, besides a simple pass-through view and a few experimental apps, it has a lot of potential. The camera's lag is currently providing an unpleasant user experience, but it will become less pronounced with more powerful image-processing hardware on the horizon. Possible application could be an in-game monitor that displays the outer world in a small window or a temporary overlay, allowing the user to interact with the environment while wearing the headset. The Oculus Quest has a similar experimental AR feature based on the inside-out tracking cameras. A big advantage for developers is the fact that the Unreal console can be directly accessed by using the four-finger touch gesture on the screen (see Figure 5-3).

Figure 5-3. *Opening the console (photo by C. Hillmann)*

On standalone headsets, this is obviously not possible because of the lack of direct screen access. The Gear VR's controller is flatter than the Oculus Go's controller, so it is easier to attach to the headset when not in use. Gear VR and Oculus Go share identical buttons and controller inputs events in Unreal, including touchpad control and a trigger button (see Figure 5-4).

Figure 5-4. *The Gear VR controller in action (photo by C. Hillmann)*

The Gear VR's motion controller includes volume control, which on the Oculus Go is on the HMD. Volume control is reserved and cannot be accessed by the developer in Unreal, which is also true for the Oculus home button. This fact requires workarounds when setting up a presentation, where the user should be prevented from accidentally hitting the home button to be pushed into the Oculus home environment. A typical example would be a trade show with a VR product presentation. The Oculus home environment would break the brand-focused presentation. Because it is not possible to disable the button from the software side, VR marketing providers have been finding solutions such as taping over it, or using 3D-printed covers to disable access to the home button.

The Gear VR comes without headphones, and as a result, most users don't go through the extra step to connect a headphone to the smartphone's headjack, as it adds extra effort to the already involved setup of sliding the phone into the headset position. This fact cuts a lot of users out from one of the most substantial ingredients of a complete VR experience: spatial audio.

Nevertheless, the Gear VR has been the initial driver of premium mobile VR. Between its early developers edition in 2014 until 2018, the HMD was reportedly sold around ten million times. That number has to be taken with caution, as most Gear VR headsets were given away in promos, bundles, special deals and giveaways and ended up being unused. Samsung has noticeably changed its efforts in promoting the headset. Until 2017, it was part of major ad campaigns, store promotions and a talking point at industry keynotes. Soon after the Oculus Go was announced, Samsung toned down its efforts to actively promote the device.

With around 10 million headsets in consumer hands, the Gear VR is currently the biggest player in the VR world. The question is whether headsets sold is the right metric to gauge the active user base. User numbers are difficult to get, as most VR companies don't publish them. But it is possible to get an idea by sampling online media activity numbers that reflect consumer engagement.

Take, for example, the user numbers for the Gear VR and the Oculus Go Reddit group activity in a mid-November 2018 snapshot: r/OculusGo had 7.1k subscribers (91 online) while r/GearVR had 28.8k subscribers (50 online).

Considering that the Oculus Go sales are estimated to be between one-half to one million vs. ten million Samsung Gear VR sold until 2018, the Reddit activity numbers gives a clear indicator that the Oculus Go appears to be a stickier product with consumers, as apparently a lot of Gear VR headsets are seldom used by their owners.

The reasons for that are obvious. Even though the Gear VR remains a premium mobile HMD—considering the fact that the latest generation of smartphones deliver better battery life, less overheating and overall top-end mobile graphics performance—it is the so-called friction funnel, of having to set up the HMD using the phone, that keeps users away from using it on a regular basis. The instant-VR effect that the frictionless Oculus Go provides—integrated headphones included—is clearly a step closer in winning over consumers.

The Oculus Go in Comparison

The Oculus Go is based on a Snapdragon 821 processor. In terms of raw processing power, it sits between the Snapdragon 820 used in the Samsung Galaxy S7 smartphone and the Snapdragon 835 used in the Samsung Galaxy S8 and the Oculus Quest. Considering the fact that the Oculus Go is highly optimized for VR performance, it is actually closer to the Samsung Galaxy S8 than the S7, considering performance and heat management.

Developers that want to ship on all available Gear VR versions have to make sure to profile their apps on the lowest-performing hardware which is the Samsung S6. For a lot of mobile VR titles with more complex graphics, the Samsung Galaxy S7 is the baseline. For that reason, numerous titles exclude the Samsung Galaxy S6 via the minimum system requirement in the Oculus store, even though there are still larger numbers of the device in use worldwide. When the Samsung Galaxy S7 was introduced in 2016, an experimental demo using the Vulkan API was circulated to demonstrate the new generation of graphics capabilities using the Snapdragon 820. When the Snapdragon 821 was introduced later in 2016, it was considered an optimization and complement to the original design first introduced with the 820.

Due to the efforts of Oculus, the Android environment is optimized to focus solely on delivering a premium VR experience. Android services typical for a mobile phone have been stripped away to make this performance possible. Due to the fact that Oculus modified the typical Android setup, some services (such as Google Play) are not available on the Oculus standalone platforms. There are a number of third-party plugins and tools in the Unreal marketplace that rely on Google Play Services; they do not work with Oculus standalone devices for this reason.

Compared to the Gear VR lineup with compatible smartphones, the Oculus Go comes with a fast-switch LCD screen that provides better clarity than the Gear VR OLED screens. The Oculus Go also comes with optimized Fresnel lens and a larger field of view of 110 degrees, comparable to the Oculus Rift, as opposed to the 101 degrees the Gear VR provides.

Overall, there are numerous small improvements that make the Oculus Go much more consumer-friendly, including small design improvements for the controller, such as a much more comfortable form factor (see Figure 5-5).

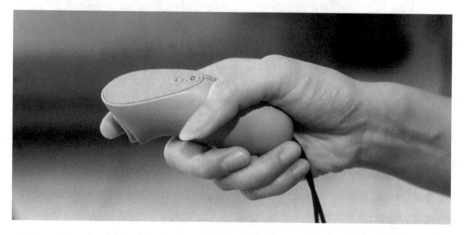

Figure 5-5. *The Oculus Go controller (photo by C. Hillmann)*

The Oculus Go controller has been labeled as the best 3DOF controller available. The trigger balances the grip much better than on the Gear VR and more comfortable ergonomics adds to a better user experience. Input actions are the same as on the Gear VR (see Figure 5-6).

Figure 5-6. *VR model of the controller (Republique VR in-game use)*

The accessory market for standalone VR is expected to pick up as the market grows. While currently carry bags, foam replacements, gamepads and battery packs dominate the market, there are a number of useful add-ons to enhance the overall experience. Noise-canceling headphones, such as the Bose QC, help to focus in a noisy environment, and wearable gear, such as the SUBPAC tactile audio system, enhances lower-frequency perception, especially on high-impact sounds (see Figure 5-7).

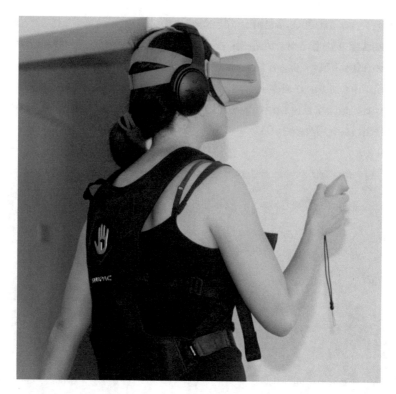

Figure 5-7. *Go with headphones and haptic vest (photo by C. Hillmann)*

Audio enhancements can add an additional level of immersion for shooting related titles by adding premium audio fidelity and haptic low-frequency vibration to the experience.

The Oculus Quest

The Oculus Quest is full 6DOF headset with inside-out tracking, allowing a high-performance wireless room-scale experience. Oculus has communicated that great emphasis is put into strict curation of highly performance-optimized games that take full advantage of the Snapdragon 835 processor. The controller's input events are identical to the Oculus

Rift's touch controllers, making it easier for Rift developers to port an optimized title to the standalone platform. The Quest controllers have a different tracking design than the Oculus touch controllers, due to the requirements of the inside-out system, but in terms of ergonomics and haptic interaction, the buttons are identical to the touch controllers of the Oculus Rift (see Figure 5-8).

Figure 5-8. *The Oculus Rift's touch controllers (photo by C. Hillmann)*

The Oculus Quest is clearly positioned as a gaming device as opposed to the Oculus GO, which has a focus on media. A statement by Oculus defined the projected consumer positioning for the Oculus Go as 80% media and 20% gaming usage, while for the Oculus Quest, the projected usage is 80% gaming and 20% media.

Comparing the Technical Specs

The comparison of the technical specs of the Gear VR, the Oculus Go, and the Oculus Quest shows some similarities and a number of distinct differences.

Gear VR using the Samsung Galaxy S9

- *Resolution*: Maximum 2960×1440 pixel AMOLED display, 60Hz refresh rate (the Gear VR is not using the entire screen)

- *Processor*: Snapdragon 845

- *Tracking*: 3DOF, Gyroscope, accelerometer and magnetometer

- *Motion controller*: One 3DOF

- *Audio*: Headphone jack or smartphone internal audio

- *Field of view*: 101 degrees

- *Storage*: 64GB–256GB

- *Extra benefits*: Extended battery life, MicroSD to extend onboard storage, focal adjustment

Oculus Go

- *Resolution*: 2560×1440 LCD display, 60–72Hz refresh rate

- *Processor*: Snapdragon 821

- *Tracking*: 3DOF, gyroscope, accelerometer, and magnetometer

- *Motion controller*: One 3DOF

- *Audio*: Fully integrated open ear, spatial audio

- *Field of view*: 110 degrees

- *Storage*: 32GB–64GB

- *Extra benefits*: Optimized Fresnel lens

Oculus Quest

- *Resolution*: 2880×1600 twin OLED display, 72Hz refresh rate

- *Processor*: Snapdragon 835

- *Tracking*: 6DOF, inside-out tracking, room-scale

- *Motion controller*: Two 6DOF

- *Audio*: Fully integrated open ear, spatial audio with enhanced bass

- *Field of view*: 110 degrees

- *Storage*: 64GB

- *Extra benefits*: Optimized Fresnel lens, IPD adjustment, internal cooling fan

Comparing the base specs, it becomes obvious that between the Gear VR and the Oculus Go, the latter offers the more superior VR experience, due to the larger field of view, the enhanced lenses, crisper image quality, and the integrated spatial audio. The Gear VR holds an edge when it comes to battery life and storage, two factors that may be important when setting up a commercial experience area, where a large number of devices have to be managed.

The Oculus Quest is really in a league of its own, due to the full 6DOF room-scale tracking capabilities. While clearly targeted at games, the 6DOF features can also benefit business and learning applications, providing more natural environments and object-interaction capabilities.

Button Mapping Overview

Let's look at a button mapping comparison between the Gear VR (A), the Oculus Go (B) , and the Oculus Quest (C) for the right hand. The Gear VR and the Oculus Go use only one controller on either the right or left hand, while on the Oculus Quest both hands can be equipped with controllers and therefore the amount of available buttons is doubled.

In the overview, we see that the trigger button (1) is the same for each controller, the touchpad (2) is identical on both the Gear and the Go, while on the Quest it is an analog stick (8). Both the touchpad and the analog stick generate the same axis data output. The Gear and the Go each have a face button (3), typically used to go back, but freely assignable. The Quest has two face buttons (5, 6) and a side trigger (7), typically used to equip in-game items. All three headsets have the reserved Oculus home button that cannot be assigned in Unreal (4), and the Gear VR has the volume controls on the motion controller that is also reserved and not available for assignment in Unreal (see Figure 5-9).

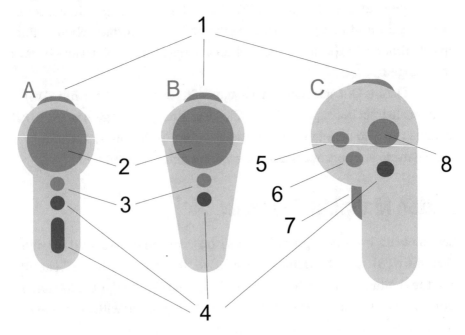

Figure 5-9. *The Gear VR (A), Oculus Go (B) , and Quest (C) buttons (right hand)*

In Unreal, the input events are assigned as follows.

1. MotionController (R) Trigger

2. MotionController (R) Thumbstick

3. MotionController (R) Face Button1

4. Reserved

5. MotionController (R) Face Button2

6. MotionController (R) Face Button1

7. MotionController (R) Grip1

8. MotionController (R) Thumbstick

Thumbstick click event are MotionController (R) Thumbstick up/ down, left/right, while OculusTouch (R) Thumbstick CapTouch input events provide touch interaction with an axis value.

By looking at the button mapping comparison, we see that there is a good amount of consistency across all devices. This fact makes it easy to test gameplay on the Oculus Rift before deploying to Android. Most developers set up a separate game-mode for testing on the Rift. This game-mode is set up to simulate the gameplay for the final Android version. Once ready to deploy, the game-mode is swapped out to the actual Android development version.

Setting the Handedness

As Gear VR and Oculus Go have only one motion controller, the user can set his handedness preference in the device's settings. The user settings allow you to switch between a left-hand and a right-hand preference (see Figure 5-10).

Figure 5-10. *Setting handedness in the device settings*

When developing, we typically set up all interactions for one hand first, to makes sure everything functions the way we intended it to. Before we finalize the application, we have to make sure both hands are set up, thus allowing the user to switch handedness in the final application. To enable that, we just add the additional hand input, in this case left hand, as an additional input event (see Figure 5-11).

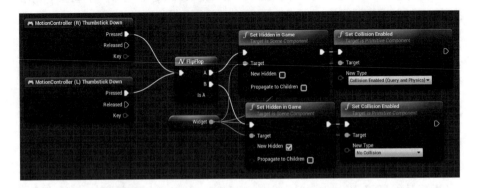

Figure 5-11. *Making sure both hands have an input events*

An alternative way to streamline all input events is to set up the engine input in the project settings for both controllers (see Figure 5-12).

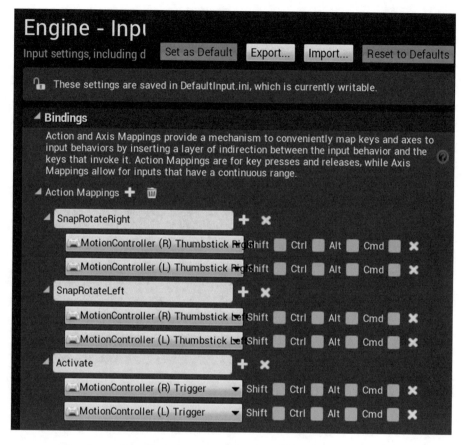

Figure 5-12. *Unifying input events in the engine input project settings*

With both hands ready to go, we now have to check which hand is active in the device defined by the user's system settings. To do that, we extend the line of execution from the begin play event in the VR pawn's event graph to do a branch condition check, to see if the device is tracked with the left hand. If it is, the user has set his handedness preference to the left hand, so we set the motion source to left; if it is not tracked on the left hand, we set the motion source to right (see Figure 5-13).

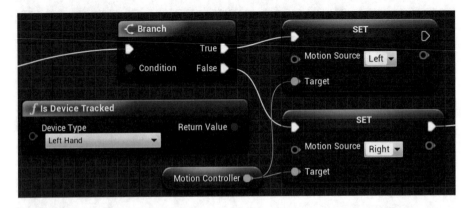

Figure 5-13. *Setting the motion source*

With these settings in place, the user can now switch between left and right hands in the device's system settings, to get the same interaction on either hand selected.

Special Requirements for the Gear VR

When developing for the Gear VR, we have to take into consideration that an OSIG signature file is needed that ties the Samsung smartphone to the application. The signature file can be generated online in the Oculus developer account and requires the adb device ID. The Generator tool is available under Develop ➤ Tools ➤ OSIG Generator (see Figure 5-14).

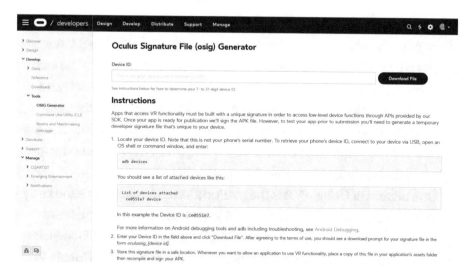

Figure 5-14. *Generating a signature file for the Gear VR*

The generated file has to be stored in the Unreal Engine directory: UE4 install location ➤ Engine ➤ Build ➤ Android ➤ Java ➤ Assets. Once the application is ready for distribution and app store submission, the OSOG file should be removed from the final APK file, by checking *Remove Oculus signature files from Distribution APK* in the advanced APK packaging section of the project settings.

Comparing Other Standalone VR HMDs

In our roundup, we had a strong focus on Oculus mobile and standalone HMDs for the reason that Oculus and Samsung cover the vast majority of the market and due to the fact that Oculus offers the most complete lineup of standalone headsets. In addition to the overall numbers of distributed HMDs, Oculus has also shown a strong commitment to the platform and its ecosystem.

If we compare the overall industry presence of Oculus with the offerings of Google VR, it becomes clear that virtual reality has a lower priority within Google's strategic positioning, noticeably due to the lack of VR-specific programming at industry events such as Google I/O and other opportunities to support Google's own VR lineup. Even though, very capable devices such as the 6DOF Lenovo Mirage solo HMD and the excellent plugin support in Unreal would make it a strong contender for high-end mobile and standalone VR applications.

One benefit of Google VR is the platform's consistency since the early cardboard versions and that Google VR apps remain largely backward compatible. Nevertheless, the low-ranking commitment from Google lets developers take a cautious position regarding the outlook for Google VR.

The other big name in VR—Vive—has laid out a very convincing roadmap for standalone VR with its premium device, the Vive Focus (see Figure 5-15). Previously only available in the Chinese market, the Vive Focus launched as a high-end standalone HMD targeting the enterprise market.

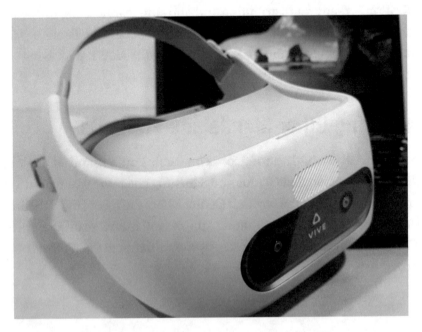

Figure 5-15. *The Vive Focus (photo by C. Hillmann)*

The Vive Focus packs a lot of innovation into similar hardware specs as the Oculus Quest, while 6DOF tracked motion controllers have only been added as an extended feature, with less reach than the Oculus Quest's four dedicated wide-angle inside-out tracking solution.

The Vive Wave Unreal SDK has not been officially integrated with Unreal Engine, so for that reason additional steps are required to set up the Unreal development environment using the Vive Wave SDK and enable the Vive Wave Unreal plugin to allow access to the Vive Wave lists of features.

The Pico Neo is another Chinese 6DOF standalone HMD based on the Vive Wave SDK and in a similar bracket of hardware specs and features. As the Vive Wave is an open source API aiming to be the standard for Chinese manufacturers, these headsets are only the first two of more to come as the Wave platform matures.

Overall, when looking at documentation, integration with Unreal and resources, Oculus is currently the most accessible and cost-efficient choice for developers in the western hemisphere.

VR HMD Types, Use Cases, and Markets

Having looked at the tech specs and overall conceptual differences, let us now take a look how these different concepts are being used in consumer and business situations. Which applications have been proven sticky after the initial wave of novelty has faded off? Even though VR can be considered a niche, it is an important component in major shifts on the consumer side and a key application for disruptive enterprises innovation. Let's look at the macro trends that will impact the future of VR for consumers and businesses and how mobile and standalone VR headsets will fit in.

Consumer VR and the Experience Economy

One of the biggest trends in consumer marketing is the "experience economy". Marketing experts have noticed a long-term shift in consumer behavior toward valuing experience more than tangible goods. For that reason, advertising agencies are building *brand experiences*. This evolution of marketing has, for example, impacted retail, whereby flagship stores are not primarily a place to sell goods but a place to experience a brand.

In the end, the consumer is free to buy merchandise on any channel—online or offline; but to capture the consumer's mind, a brand must use a bigger idea—involving brand storytelling and brand experience—to communicate its unique message. The experience economy is about experiencing brands and seeing the experience itself as a value. On its ways to becoming more consumer friendly, VR will play an increasingly important role in communicating a brand's journey with the consumer.

The high impact of immersive brand storytelling is one of the great promises in VR marketing. Early success stories in this trend are try-before-you-buy VR presentations of new vehicles and remote viewings of real estate or vacation rental properties. Very often, experience areas are part of a new product launch, where consumers can familiarize themselves with the ins-and-outs of new product features in a VR presentation.

Gaming is currently the biggest application area for VR and we can expect that to spill over into education and business applications, by gamification of marketing material and brand experiences. The fitness industry will see a big move into immersive gear and gamification-enabled exercise equipment once VR HMDs become better suited in exercise situations.

Taking the overall trend into consideration, mobile VR such as the Gear VR is a strong contender to supply VR experience areas as typically used in marketing, due to the long battery life and memory expansion that the latest-generation Samsung smartphones enables.

The Oculus Go is an efficient presentation tool for smaller groups and ideal for sharing design concepts with consumers. 6DOF standalone VR HMDS such as the Oculus Quest, however, are best suited for large model reviews and real estate applications with strong spatial features. Examples would be designs where the change of the positional viewing position allows you to verify concepts, such as looking under, over, or behind walls.

VR for Business, Enterprise, and the Impact of Industry 4.0

The disruptive shift that is transforming the enterprise world is called Industry 4.0, and VR plays a key role in it. Industry 4.0 is the umbrella term for the digitalization and connectivity revolution in the data-driven manufacturing processes. It is referred to as the *fourth industrial revolution,* connecting a number of key technology trends as drivers of a new area of increased innovation and productivity. Some of them are digitalization, big data, artificial intelligence, Internet of Things, and cloud computing.

One of the key concepts within the Industry 4.0 innovation areas is that of the digital twin. The digital twin is a virtual representation of a physical system, with the goal of collecting and understanding simulation data, to communicate concepts and provide a training resource. Communicating concepts and the possibility of creating a training resource with digital replicas have become important areas of application for mobile VR.

To address the growing enterprise market, a dedicated Unreal version called Unreal Studio was launched with tools for CAD data exchange and additional visualization tools, to enable an optimized real-time graphics visualization pipeline for the industrial design and manufacturing process. Unreal Studio provides dedicated tools for converting DCC and CAD data to high-performance real-time assets. This allows users to accelerate the creation of presentation assets for design reviews and optimize iterative processes, including bringing optimized assets to a standalone VR headset.

VR visualization in the design process is a natural extension of the traditional design communication practice. Originally, product designers, architects, and concept artists would communicate concepts with rendered 2D images or flythrough videos. Being able to experience a design concept in VR is the natural next logical step to communicate more efficiently and with higher impact.

Industry 4.0 digitalization, and the concept of the digital twin, plays a similarly important role when it comes to training staff on new equipment. Typically, training on the actual equipment means expensive downtime, as the equipment cannot be operated until the staff is fully trained to use it. In cases like this, the digital twin is an effective way to bypass this costly bottleneck and train the staff on a digital copy of the actual equipment. For example, a piece of machinery is converted from CAD data to real-time assets and equipment functions are overlaid with interactive tool tips and animations to demonstrate its abilities and use.

The Oculus Go has been successfully used for training applications in similar scenarios. A large department store chain, for example, had supplied its training centers with 50 thousand headsets to train staff on a new packing machine. This allowed the store to avoid the bottleneck after the equipment installation, thereby guaranteeing no downtime. Furthermore, the realistic immersive simulation of the equipment using VR proved to be superior and much more efficient than conventional training using videos, images, and printed manuals.

Mobile and standalone VR will play an increasing role in this area. Immersive simulation, training, and education are an essential part of the Industry 4.0 revolution and will continue to be part of the innovation of how humans interact with information.

The current lineup of available mobile and standalone VR headsets has already played a role in this major trend. The Oculus Go has proven itself to be efficient in this area, due partially to the fact that it is affordable and easy to set up and use. As VR continues to increase its role in the digital design and manufacturing process, so will custom industry-specific solutions. We can expect better customization features for VR headsets in the future, including a kiosk mode to allow custom-branded VR headsets that start up with customized splash screen bypassing the firmware.

Conclusion

In this chapter, we have looked at the differences of the Gear VR, the Oculus Go, and the Oculus Quest. We compared the hardware specs and the features that differentiate the individual line of HMDs. We compared the button input events on all controller types and how to switch hand with single motion controllers. We then compared the Samsung and Oculus lineup to other standalone VR HMD options. Finally, we looked at how the headsets are being used by consumers and businesses and where each headset has its best use case based on features.

CHAPTER 6

Creating an Interactive VR Presentation

In this chapter, we build the basic components needed for a VR presentation and go through all production steps from start to finish. These steps include blocking out the scene idea, building geometry and UVs, creating tiling materials, sculpting the main model and retopologizing it, creating tileable materials, lighting the scene in Unreal, and building an interactive menu to activate a scene animation and property changes on the presentation model. The goal is to give a quick overview of the most important steps when building a VR presentation that is typical for a B2B project.

VR presentations have become a natural extension of the 3D visualization process and are increasingly used by businesses to give clients the opportunity to review design iterations and options. Typical examples are real estate previsualizations where the VR showcase lets the clients change materials to review different options for interiors, such as wall colors and floor finishings. Another example would be an industrial designer discussing model options with his client through a VR presentation.

Other use cases are training apps where employees are trained on new equipment before it actually becomes available. This approach is a typical application in the context of the Industry 4.0 philosophy, where a digital twin of a physical object represents a virtual copy for simulation and training.

© Cornel Hillmann 2019
C. Hillmann, *Unreal for Mobile and Standalone VR*,
https://doi.org/10.1007/978-1-4842-4360-2_6

We will focus on the core components that bring this approach together. These core components are a pleasant-looking environment with a showroom character and an interactive presentation model that can be accessed through a user interface in the VR scene.

Once we understand how these components are built, we are able to expand the basic concept with larger environments and more detailed models and more complex interactions.

Project Description

Our objective is to create an interactive presentation of a 3D model in VR. Let's propose a situation. We are a design studio and are hired to develop the shape of a new long-distance jet ski model. Our client wants to see and experience the progression of the design process, including the ability to interactively review model property options, such as color variation. He also would like to see a moveable part animated, so that the interior details of the model can be revealed.

The objective is to work through different iterations of the model starting with a low poly model in the beginning that communicates the basic concept. To make the scene more realistic, we decided to present the model in a warehouse-type, factory-showroom environment. This idea communicates that the model is not yet ready to be shown in public, as it is still in the internal review process. The model is docked on a stand as it would be at the first public reveal when it is shown at a trade-show floor.

Blocking out the Scene

We start out with nothing but the initial rough sketch of the first concept idea. Before we even start modeling anything, we move to the very first step, which means blocking out the scene in the Unreal editor. Starting with an empty scene, we use the Geometry Brush tools under the Mode tab in the right panel. At this point, we have already set up the project to run with the Oculus Go and are using the flexible teleportation locomotion mechanics and motion controller setup that were established in Chapter 4. To use the same Blueprints, we copied the Content folder of that project into our new project and established the project settings for an Android project, as we did in Chapter 4.

The blocking phase is an important first step in establishing the environment and its proportions. It lets us evaluate if the room feels right in its dimension, for example, if the ceiling is high enough and the overall dimension feels appropriate for the project. We will use simple geometry shapes to sketch out the rough environment.

In addition to geometry, we add a few static lights to review how the room will look with indoor lighting. Having the Oculus Go connected as a launch device allows us to test the scene on the Go and quickly move around in the blocked out environment to review its dimensions. We use the Unreal cube geometry brush as a block-out tool, scale it into shape, duplicate it a few time to create walls floor and ceiling, plus any additional room features. To block out openings such as doors and windows, we switch the cube geometry brush to negative volume and cut out the spaces where we need them (see Figure 6-1).

Figure 6-1. *Blocking out the scene with geometry and negative volume*

Refining the Scene in Blender

Once the basic scene dimension is blocked out and tested on the Oculus Go, we export the geometry as an FBX file from the File ➤ Export Selected menu. In Blender we import the FBX file and place the geometry in a background layer with wireframe shading. This allows us to recreate much more efficient geometry based on the imported pieces. Our goal is not only to make the geometry more efficient for UV textures and lightmaps, but also add occasional detail, like railings, door and window frames, to make the room features more convincing (see Figure 6-2).

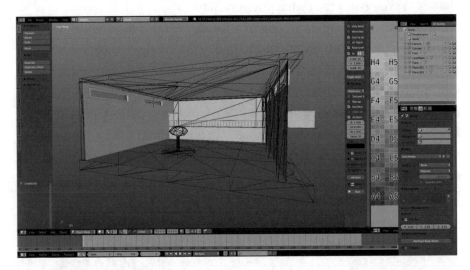

Figure 6-2. *Re-creating clean geometry based on imported FBX concept*

To view and edit the room interior, we *flip* the geometry normals, so that they are facing inward, and we enable Backface Culling under the Shading menu, and then assign materials IDs to the different parts of the interior model. The next step is to create a UV map that allows us to spread a tiling material evenly across each part. For the wall, we have to make sure all wall UV islands have the same orientation. We are planning to create a

PBR material with tiling textures for the floor and wall, so we need to verify the correct positioning using a UV color grid under the New Image options in the Blender UV/Image editor (see Figure 6-3).

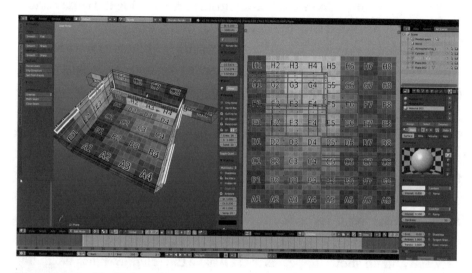

Figure 6-3. *Verifying the correct UV layout*

We are now ready to export the entire scene as an FBX file for later use in Unreal. Next, we look into creating tiling texture materials for the floor and walls.

Creating Scene Materials Using Substance Designer

Substance Designer is the de-facto industry standard for creating environment textures. In Chapter 2, we looked at how to use Substance Painter to texture props as part of the asset production pipeline using a single texture map. For very large assets such as environments, buildings and interiors, this approach would not work, as the texture size would be too large to be efficient. For that reason, we have to take a different approach and create textures that are tileable across large model sections in a convincing way. Using a node-based procedural approach, Substance Designer lets us customize and tweak any possible aspect of the final PBR material appearance that we can build from scratch using the large node library that is provided with the application.

Substance is very well integrated in most digital content creation (DCC) tools, including Unreal. The Substance plugin in Unreal lets you tweak exposed parameters, even at runtime, on the Windows platform.

At the time this book was published, the Substance plugin is not yet supported on Android platforms, even though this is on the roadmap. That means we have to export the generated PBR textures from the Substance Designer application and create the material manually in our project. In case we need to change, tweak, or rearrange anything in the final texture result, we just have to go back into Substance Designer re-export and replace the textures in our Unreal material. It is basically an extra step in between and no showstopper, as we still have the full power and flexibility of Substance Designer at our disposal.

The Substance Designer Workflow

In this section, we quickly go over what the important ingredients of a substance are, as an in-depth tutorial would require its own volume. Let's look at the first substance that we are using for this project—the wooden floor texture (see Figure 6-4).

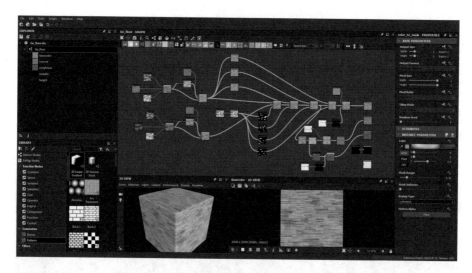

Figure 6-4. *Setting up a floor material in Substance Designer*

We create a material with PBR outputs by combining a number of different noise generators using a Blend node, followed by a colorization step in which we replaced the grayscale with a color range and combined it with a background color (see Figure 6-5).

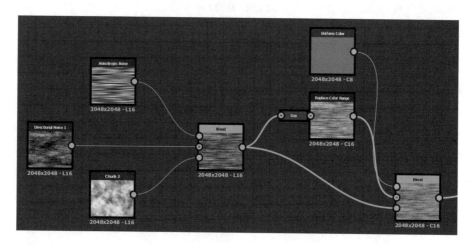

Figure 6-5. *Setting up the wood grain in Substance Designer*

175

The other important ingredient next to the initial grain is the tiling. To make the tiling less obvious, we have to create sufficient variation within the individual texture that will be used for tiling later. To accomplish this, we create a gradient map from a Tile Generator node and generate a number of different offset patterns by selecting grayscale value from the grayscale patterns (see Figure 6-6).

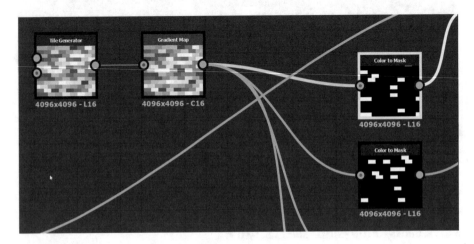

Figure 6-6. *Creating tile offset patterns*

For the grout, we introduce a brick generator with the same tile values as the original tile generator and use it for the normal map, while blending the inverted brick texture with the color map (see Figure 6-7). Tweaking the grayscale values with luminosity and contrast in combination with the grout input through the brick generator allows us to produce the final normal and roughness map.

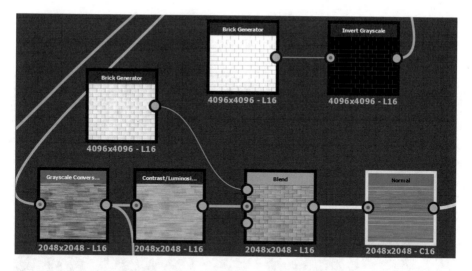

Figure 6-7. *Creating grout with the brick generator*

Since the original texture size was set up for 4096×4096, to zoom in and review close-up details, we scale back the final output to 2048×2048, right-click the Substance in the Explorer panel, and choose Export As Bitmaps. The result is a wooden floor texture set that is appropriate for a factory showroom.

For the wall texture, we are looking for a rustic large brick look that could be found in a typical factory showroom (see Figure 6-8).

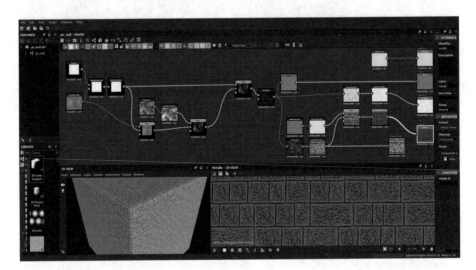

Figure 6-8.   *The wall texture in Substance Designer*

Here again, we focus on the individual brick part at first, using a Polygon node, combining it with a Fractal node, and blending it with a spot noise generator after increasing contrast and luminosity (see Figure 6-9).

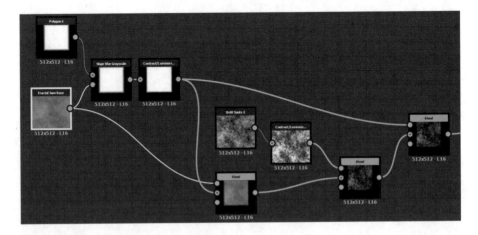

Figure 6-9.   *Generating the bricks*

To generate a random brick pattern, we'll use it as an input for the Tile Random node (see Figure 6-10).

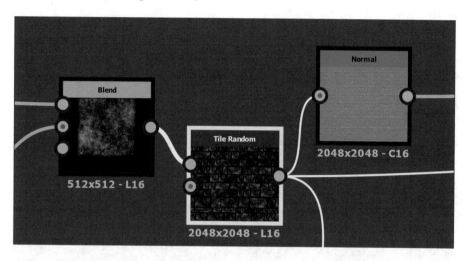

Figure 6-10. *Generating the brick pattern*

In the last section, we generate a roughness texture by inverting and level-correcting the grayscale pattern output. The metalness map is created by combining a light noise blended with ambient occlusion from the tile generator. We also keep a separate ambient occlusion output to be used in the final material (see Figure 6-11).

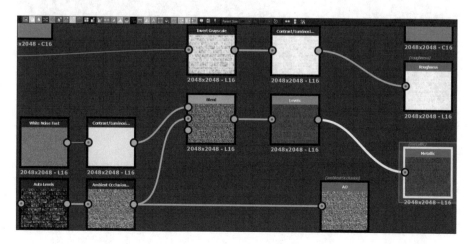

Figure 6-11. *Generating roughness, metalness, and ambient occlusion*

Once everything is set up, we make sure that the export size is 2048×2048, right-click the Substance in the Explorer tab, and select Export As Bitmaps.

Creating the Low Poly Mesh for the Jet Ski Object

Starting with a sphere in ZBrush, we sketch out a concept sculpt using mostly the Move, Dam Standard, and Trim Dynamic brushes. The Sculptris Pro and Dynamesh features allow us to reshape the mesh until we come to a satisfying result (see Figure 6-12).

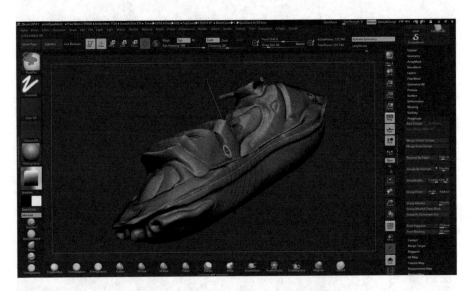

Figure 6-12. Sculpting a rough concept mesh in ZBrush

Our goal up to this point is to create the right base shape and volume. We will use the high polygon model in Blender as a starting point to simplify the concept and create a low polygon version using the retopology tools in Blender.

Once we finalize the retopology process using the commercial plugin RetopoFlow, we add a stand for the model and separate the low polygon model into separate parts, because we are planning to animate the hood of the jet ski in Unreal later (see Figure 6-13).

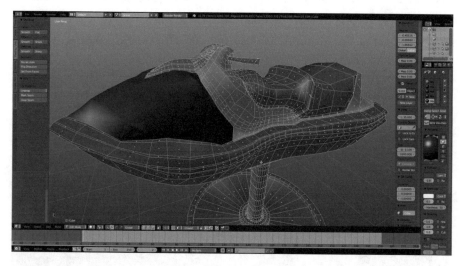

Figure 6-13. *The low polygon model separated into two parts*

Replacing the Blocked out Meshes with the Actual Scene Objects

In the last step before exporting, we position the jet ski and the stand inside the showroom. Finally, we export the entire scene as an FBX. In Unreal, we import the FBX file with drag and drop into the content browser. From the Import options, we deselect Skeletal Mesh and Auto Generate Collision from the Mesh section and leave the other options as is. Our goal is to create a customized collision mesh at a later point, so it is most efficient for our scene.

To place the scene in the Unreal editor, we delete the blocked-out geometry, select all parts of the new mesh, and drop it all into the scene. Dropping all parts together makes sure that the relative offset of all mesh objects stays intact. If the scene is slightly off center, we zero out the position in the Transform panel, while everything is selected. We should now have the factory showroom with the jet ski on a stand at exactly the same position as the original blocked-out concept (see Figure 6-14).

Figure 6-14. *The imported mesh with material ID colors in the editor*

Setting Materials, Collision Mesh, and Lightmap Resolution

To apply our substance output textures to the model, we have to create a material for the wall and the floor. We drop all of our substance texture files into the content browser, right-click, and choose Create Material under Basic Assets. The connections are with any basic PBR material obvious through the texture names. To tile the textures across the model, we connect a Tex Coord node with all textures UV input and set the tiling to 8 in each direction (see Figure 6-15).

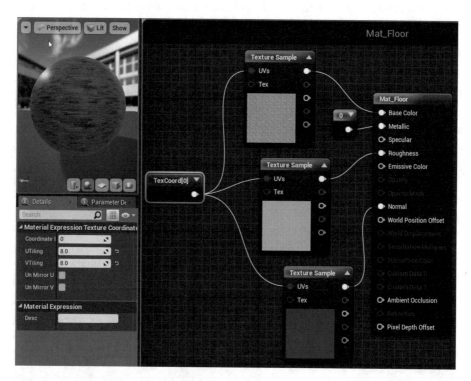

Figure 6-15. *The floor material*

We create an extra constant input for the metallic input in case we want to add a slight metalness later. For the wall material, we do the same, except that we use a three-vector constant node for the base color. Additionally, we add the ambient occlusion texture that was generated in Substance Designer, but tone it down with a Clamp node that carries the maximum output of 0.8 (see Figure 6-16).

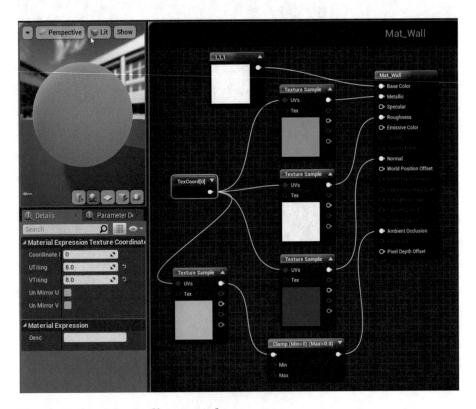

Figure 6-16. *The wall material*

We are now ready to assign the material to the main mesh. We open the mesh in the Static Mesh editor by selecting it in the outliner and selecting edit from the right-click menu. In the Model editor, we replace the materials in the two material ID slots with our substance material for the walls and the floors (see Figure 6-17).

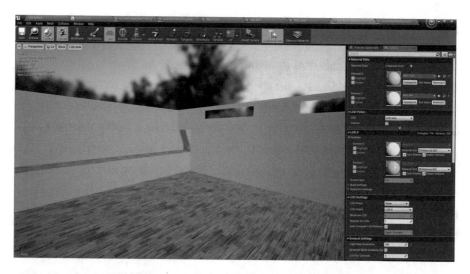

Figure 6-17. *Setting materials, collision, and lightmap in the Static Mesh editor*

From the Details tab, we scroll all the way down to the Collision section and select Use Complex Collision As Simple from the Collision Trace Behavior pull-down menu. Since our basic room mesh is fairly simple, we can use the actual geometry to generate collision with this option. In the General Settings options, we set the Lightmap Resolution to 256. The default resolution is almost always too low and results in jagged-looking shadows. We will confirm or adjust the resolution according to the result we are getting after building the lighting. We process the other mesh parts in a similar fashion, except for the railing where we use a simple box collision to cover the entire mesh.

For the door and window frames, we create simple off-white material, and for the actual jet ski we create one master material with parametric color and metalness values. From the master material, we create six different material instance colors and metalness variations to play with different color sets.

Lighting the Scene

Having set all materials and lightmap resolutions, we are now able to light the scene with point lights and spotlights. It is important to remember that, for VR we should use baked lighting wherever possible. Therefore, any object that doesn't move should be set to static object, and a light should always be set to static light unless there is a strong reason not to do so.

Unreal has a great dynamic lighting system, but for most VR scenes, it is an overkill and too expensive to use. If scene objects and lights are set to static, we get the advantage that the entire scene is completely baked, which means there is no performance cost for additional lights. In this scenario, we can add as many lights as needed for designing the overall room ambience without affecting the real-time performance, because the lighting result is completely baked into the final lightmap.

For this scene, we add a number of spotlights and where we adjust the attenuation radius and intensity in the Lights section of the Details panel and a spotlight, for which the cone radius is adjusted to get the desired result (see Figure 6-18). To update the scene, we select Build The Lighting Only from the Build menu in the top menu bar and then launch it on the Oculus Go headset to review the results.

Figure 6-18. *Adjusting the static scene lights*

Having set all textures and lights (see Figure 6-19), let us go over some important settings to achieve the best possible render results, before moving on to the interactive setup for this project.

Figure 6-19.   *The finalized texture and lights setup for the scene*

Strategies for Achieving the Optimum Lightmap Results

The rich feature set of Unreal has numerous ways to tweak lightmap results. The precondition for good lighting results is efficient UVs. Unreal automatically creates a UV map, especially for the lightmap in the next available UV channel based on the supplied UV map, typically UV channel 1 if we have stored our own UV maps in UV channel 0. The next precondition, especially for smooth shadows, is a high-enough lightmap resolution that we set in the Static Mesh editor for the individual mesh.

Surfaces that are not visible to the user should have the lowest possible lightmap resolution; otherwise, we would waste resources here. The trade-off to increase lightmap resolutions is the increased texture memory requirement, the increased GPU bandwidth-cost of rendering a frame and an increase of build time. Decisions on how to balance the budget for texture memory has to be made on a per-project basis.

In general, it is a good idea to start in the middle range and then work our way up. The *lightmap importance volume* is an important tool to control unnecessary overhead in build times. We can drag it from the Volumes tab in the Modes panel on the left, and position and scale it in a way that the outline of the box covers the entire scene that is visible to the user. This way, we make sure outfacing or unnecessary geometry outside of the lightmass importance volume gets less priority in lightmap calculations.

For mobile and standalone VR, it is generally a best practice to bake all lighting with shadows included. If an object is movable, it is usually preferred to uncheck shadows on the object and disguise the lack of object shadows with scene-dressing techniques. If dramatic light is an important part of the scene and the movable object must have a dynamic shadow, we may turn a static light into a stationary light to generate shadows for the moveable object. In this case, we should make sure that the overall performance allows us to do that. It is in general a good idea not to exceed one single stationary light to generate dynamic shadows, if it is absolutely necessary.

It is a good idea to review the scene lights and lightmap density in the optimization viewport modes. Changing the Lit mode from the top left of the viewport to Lighting Only gives us a good overview over the light distribution in the scene. In the Lightmap Density view mode under Optimization View Modes, we can review how evenly the lightmap resolution for static meshes is distributed and adjust accordingly. Our goal is an evenly distributed texel density.

To override the lightmap resolution for all static mesh scene objects, it is possible to give a minimum-maximum range or a percentage in the Lightmap Resolution Adjustment panel in the Lighting Info dialog under the Build menu on the top toolbar.

To optimize the overall quality of the lightmap, we should change the settings from preview to production in the lighting quality settings under the Build menu. To further tweak the results, we should review the first five settings under the Lightmass tab in the World Settings menu.

Let's take a look at the settings.

- *Static Lighting Level Scale.* The default is 1.0 and gives good results. A value of 0.9 can be considered in some cases, even though build times increase dramatically.

- *Number of Indirect Lighting Bounces for Point, Spot, and Directional Lights.* The default is 3. This number can easily be increased without a major hit in build times. Anywhere around 10 is acceptable. In some cases, people use it with a value up to 100; the higher value only moderately affects build times.

- *Number of Skylight and Emissive Bounces.* The default is 1, but this can be increased without problem in conjunction with the previous setting.

- *Indirect Lighting Quality.* The default is 1 and already gives a very good result. This should be increased with caution, as it increases build times considerably. From 3 to a maximum of 6 is acceptable if the scene really requires it.

- *Indirect Lighting Smoothness.* The default is at 1 and can easily be increased to 3 if the lightmap needs smoothing in certain areas and the loss of detail is acceptable.

After tweaking the lightmap settings, fine tuning the lightmap resolution, and adjusting the light settings and overall texel density, we are able to generate the best possible baking results for our VR project.

Creating a Sequencer Animation for Interaction

One part of the interactive presentation is the ability to lift up the hood of the jet ski to reveal the engine, which is a special feature of this concept. In Blender, we separate the hood as an extra model, allowing us to animate it separately. We go to the top menu and select Add Level Sequence from the Cinematics menu.

In the New Sequencer window, we add the hood static mesh item to the left panel, set the initial location transform keyframes to the start position, move the mesh up in the scene, create another keyframe, set another keyframe after 2 seconds, and at the end copy the start keyframes to the end of the animation (see Figure 6-20). To test it, hit Play.

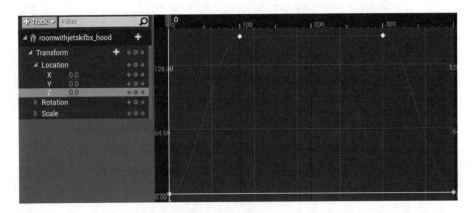

Figure 6-20. *The hood animated along the Z-axis in the sequencer*

The hood moved up, revealing the engine, stays in position for 2 seconds, and then returns to its initial position. We save the sequencer, name it *hood level sequence,* and close it. The sequence is now available for us to be triggered in the scene through an event.

Creating Interactive Elements with Widget Interaction

Widget interaction allows us to place a UMG menu widget into the 3D world using the widget component inside of a Blueprint actor. It is fast and easy to set up and can be controlled with the widget interaction component that we add to the VR pawn as another child of the motion controller. Our goal is to have a floating menu with buttons that the player can approach in the 3D environment. By activating the buttons using the motion controller trigger, we want to activate specific events in the presented object. In our case, we want to activate the hood animation with a button click and assign different material colors to the jet ski model. To assign the material change events to the model, we first have to convert the static mesh into a Blueprint actor.

Converting a Mesh to a Blueprint and Adding Custom Events

With the static mesh actor, and our jet ski model selected in the world outline, we click the blue Blueprint/Add Script button. This instantly creates a Blueprint with a static mesh component inside which holds the jet ski model.

Once we open the event graph of the Blueprint, we add three custom events and select Add Event ➤ Add Custom Event from the right-click menu. Since we want to create three different color options for the main body of the jet ski, we create three custom events, one for each color. We name each one accordingly—*setcolor1*, *setcolor2*, *setcolor3*, and connect the output with a Set Material node.

Inside the Material slot, we choose one material instance for each option. We set the element index accordingly because it is a multimaterial mesh, and input the static mesh component, which is our jet ski model, as the target (see Figure 6-21).

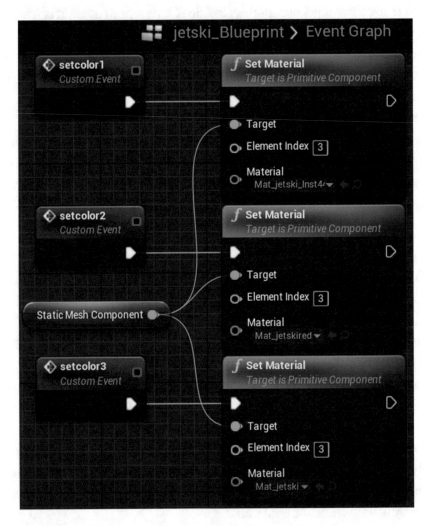

Figure 6-21. *Custom events in the Jet Ski Blueprint event graph*

Creating a UI with the UMG Widget Designer and Event Graph

Right-clicking in the content browser, we select Widget Blueprint in the user interface drop-down menu at the bottom of the menu, to create a new UMG Blueprint widget. We set a medium size of 400×200 pixel and add four buttons with a text layer (see Figure 6-22).

Figure 6-22. *Adding buttons to the UMG widget*

The UMG widget makes each button instantly available in the Graphs section of the Blueprint as a variable and an *on clicked* event. To enable the level sequence for the Show Engine button, we add a Create Level Sequence Player node and select the level sequence by name in the Level Sequence slot. We connect the outgoing pins with a sequencer Play node. To communicate with the Jet Ski Model Blueprint for the color change buttons, we need to use a Get All Actors Of Class node, where we specify our Jet Ski Blueprint in the Actor Class slot and connect the output with the custom events that we created for the respective buttons (see Figure 6-23).

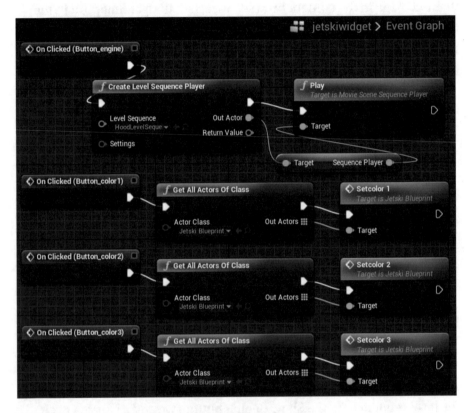

Figure 6-23. *Assigning events to widget buttons*

Setting up the Motion Controller for Widget Activation

We need to enable the motion controller to emulate a left mouse-click by using our laser pointer as an input device. To give the VR pawn access to the widget, we add the widget interaction component as another child to the motion controller using the Components tab drop-down menu.

Inside the *VR_pawn*'s event graph, we connect a Motion Controller Trigger node with a Press Pointer Key node set to Left Mouse Button, referencing our widget interaction component. We'll do the same for the Release Pointer Key node (see Figure 6-24).

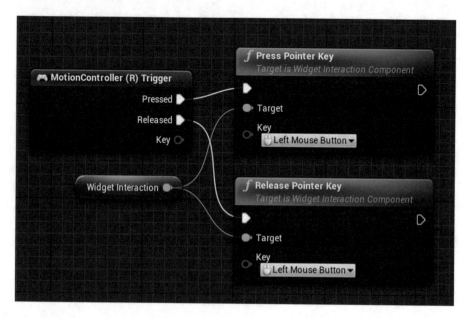

Figure 6-24. *Emulating a mouse-click with the motion controller*

Setting up the 3D Widget

We are now ready to set up the 3D scene widget that corresponds with the widget interaction component of the VR pawn. We right-click into the content browser and select Blueprint Class from the Create Basic Asset section and choose Actor from the Parent Class choices. We open the empty Blueprint actor and add the Widget component as a child to the Default Scene Root in the Components tab. Having the Widget component selected, we add our original jet ski widget under the Widget Class pull-down from the User Interface section. This places our 2D button layout as a 3D object into the Blueprint (see Figure 6-25).

Figure 6-25. *Turning a 2D widget into a 3D scene object*

Once we drop the Blueprint actor into our scene, we are able to review it as a 3D scene object that can be accessed by our VR pawn (see Figure 6-26).

Figure 6-26. *The VR scene ready for interaction*

At this point, we should build the lighting and launch the scene on the Oculus Go to evaluate the interaction. The completed VR scene allows us to move around with flexible teleportation and we can position ourselves in front of the Widget menu to select buttons to either trigger the hood removal animation sequence or the material changes on the model by activating the trigger button on the motion controller.

Conclusion

In this chapter, we created an interactive VR presentation from start to finish. We started by blocking out the scene and modeling efficient geometry with aligned UVs in Blender. We designed tiling materials for the floors and walls from scratch using Substance Designer. We built the main model by sculpting a concept in ZBrush and retopologizing it in Blender. We then set up the scene with materials and lights in Unreal.

Using the flexible teleportation and motion controller setup from Chapter 4, we added interaction by setting up a 3D scene widget with the widget interaction component and a Blueprint actor for our main model, where we set up custom events to trigger material changes on the model. We created an animation using the sequencer to lift the hood of the model to expose the engine.

Finally, we assigned buttons to the interaction and made them available as a 3D scene asset. Bringing everything together, we were able to complete an interactive model presentation on the Oculus Go as an example for a typical B2B VR project for a design client.

CHAPTER 7

An Introduction to Creating VR Game Mechanics

Introduction

In this chapter, we will focus on creating VR puzzle mechanics and Blueprint communication methods. While in Chapter 4 we used the level Blueprint to create interactions between different scene objects, we will in this chapter do all interaction between Blueprint actors without ever opening the Level editor. The advantage is a flexible system of scene components that can easily be reused in another level if required. By creating a small, fixed slot inventory menu, we can explore how we communicate with variables across various Blueprint actors to get or set values. Exploring the tools for character interaction gives us an introduction to customizing our own imported character meshes and setting them up to be controlled by Unreal's sophisticated animation and artificial intelligence (AI) system.

© Cornel Hillmann 2019
C. Hillmann, *Unreal for Mobile and Standalone VR*,
https://doi.org/10.1007/978-1-4842-4360-2_7

Project Description

The goal of this project is to introduce the most important Blueprint communication techniques and the basic groundwork to develop an interactive scene that allows the user to solve puzzles, explore the environment interactively, and overcome obstacles. The project is limited to two rooms (an overview can be seen in the bottom image of Figure 7-1). The first room has a locked door, so the user is inclined to search for the two keys that are required for the two locks to open it. One key is hidden in a drawer, while the other key is below a pile of boxes that have to be moved. The third item to find is a bomb igniter that is needed for the second room; it is also below the pile of boxes.

Once all items are found and stored in the inventory, they can be used on action items that require them. The second room is guarded by an AI-driven character that attacks the user at close range. The attacks cause the user's health to deteriorate, reflected in a UI health bar. The only way to escape the second room is to pick up sufficient health powerups, before entering the guarded area and deploying the igniter to the bomb near the second door. Only after the bomb is activated by the igniter and the explosion blows off the door and kills the guard, the room is cleared to exit.

Our strategy is to implement the game mechanics with blocked-out scene elements and simple, low-poly, stand-in geometry to have a working system where the mockups can later be replaced with more refined assets.

For this chapter's project, we will use the flexible teleportation from Chapter 4 as a base for moving around and for motion controller interaction, using the laser beam and hit actor reticle. To make things easier, we can just copy and paste the content folder from the Chapter 4 project into our new project before setting up Oculus, Android and input project settings. This way, we can easily assign the previous VR pawn with all the interaction settings to the new project.

The geometry assets needed in this scene are as follows: two keys and two locks, an igniter, a bomb, a health pickup cross item, and a guard character.

For stand-in, low-poly geometry, we can quickly sketch these items out in Blender, or use a free online source such as 3DWarehouse.SketchUp. com to download stand-in geometry in the Collada format that Blender can read for geometry cleanup and UV generation. The actual rooms with doors, we will block out using Unreal's geometry brushes. To manage the scene more easily, we will use walls without ceilings. To manage items in the inventory system, we need a rendered image of each pickup: one of each key in its distinct color and one rendered image of the igniter.

Setting up the Scene

After evaluating or creating the scene assets in Blender, we import the FBX files by drag and drop into the asset folder without materials checked and place them into the scene. To have materials for the items, we will create a master material with a parametric color channel. We then create four material instances: one with a default white color, and a red, a blue, and an orange version for the pickup items (see Figure 7-1).

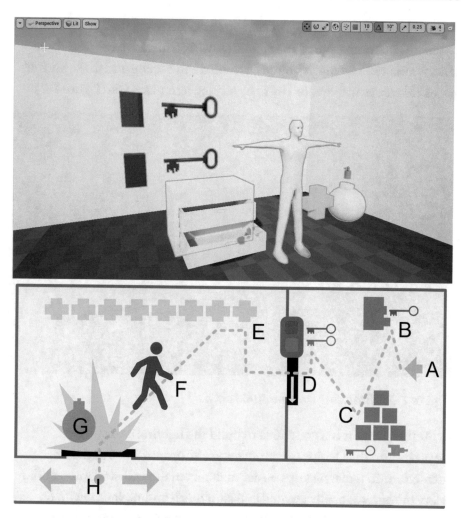

Figure 7-1. *Top: Importing 3D models and applying material instances to scene assets to start building the VR puzzle game. Bottom: The top down view in the graphic below shows the game progression starting in the first room. (A) Start. (B) Collect red key from drawer. (C) Collect blue key and igniter from under a pile of boxes. (D) Use both keys to open sliding door to the next room. (E) Collect health. (F) Survive guard attack. (G) Use igniter to activate bomb that destroys second door and kills guard. (H) Exit through destination hallway.*

To block out the scene, we scale up the floor, using the geometry brush to create two rooms with door openings using a negative volume. After that, we place a nav mesh bounds volume in the scene and make sure all accessible areas are covered by it, by scaling it in place (see Figure 7-2).

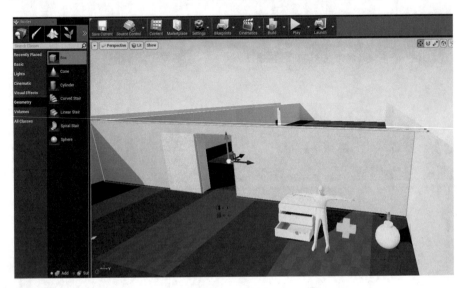

Figure 7-2. *Blocking out the two rooms*

At this point, it is a good idea to build the lighting and launch the project on the Oculus Go to review scale, proportions, and item interaction. To make pickups easier to detect in the collision interaction, delete the automatically created collision mesh and replace it with a collision capsule, from the Collision menu in the Unreal Mesh editor. The character mesh is at this point only a stand-in to review scale. It will be replaced entirely with skinned mesh and skeleton at a later point.

Using Blueprint Interfaces

Our next goal is to make the scene items interactive by using Blueprint Interfaces. By setting up a Blueprint Interface, we are able to trigger events within scene actors by using our motion controller setup. To create a Blueprint interface, right-click into the content browser and select Blueprint interface from the Create Advanced Asset menu.

All we need to do here is give the Blueprint a name, in this case Interaction Interface, open it, and add two functions. The first function is named *interaction*. We assign it an input named Controller, and we select Scene Component as the type. We call the second function *end interaction* and assign it the same input as the first function (see Figure 7-3).

Figure 7-3. *Two functions of the Blueprint interface*

Next, we have to implement the Blueprint interface to our controller inside the VR pawn Blueprint. To call the Blueprint interface functions, we extend the line of execution that we set up in Chapter 4 for teleportation (see Figure 4-46 and 4-47). Instead of passing the controller's input *activate* directly to the Set Actor Location node, we pull in a branch to verify if the location is actually a valid teleport destination. If it is not, then we can try to call the Blueprint interface on the hit actor.

The Interaction message as indicated by the letter symbol became available after we created the two functions inside of the Blueprint Interface and saved it. It should be noted that the Blueprint Interface only fires if it is actually implemented in the actor. If not, simply nothing happens.

With the interaction interface, we are also sending along the *input scene component* that we created. In this case, we hooked up the controller input to the static mesh component of our VR pawn that is actually used to generate the hit events by using the line trace by channel that we set up in Chapter 4.

The last step is to define the target actor, which in this case is the actual hit actor, as by result of the line trace (see Figure 7-4). We will also include the press key emulation for the widget interaction component that we used in Chapter 6 (see Figure 6-24). We add the component as a child of the controller mesh. It allows us to interact with UMG menu widgets in the scene.

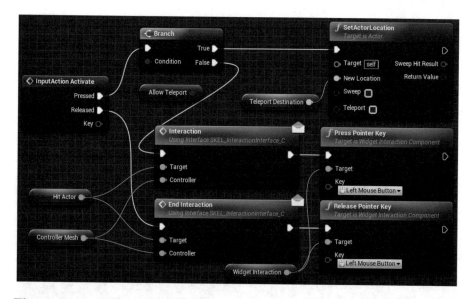

Figure 7-4. *Calling the Blueprint Interface message in the VR pawn Blueprint*

We now have to wire up the hit actor Blueprint with the Blueprint Interface to allow the communication between the different actor classes to fire off events. Our target is a simple cube. We want to pick it up, throw it around, and drop it anywhere in the scene. The idea is to create obstacles in the scene, where the player has to move boxes around to search for a missing pickup item. At this point, the cube that we dropped into the scene is a simple static mesh item. Our first step is to convert the static mesh object into a Blueprint actor class, by selecting the asset in the world outliner and then hitting the blue Blueprint/Add Script button in the Details panel.

Once the new Blueprint actor class has been created, we open its event graph, select the static mesh component, and enable Simulate Physics in the Details panel. This action automatically makes the object a movable item. Activating Simulate Physics is important because we want this item to interact with the environment, such as world gravity and other scene objects collisions, when we drop it or let it bounce against a wall, for example.

For this actor to receive Blueprint interface calls, we first need to add the interface to the class settings. On the Details panel under Class Settings, we find the Interfaces tab, which allows us to add a previously created interface as our Interaction Blueprint interface (see Figure 7-5).

Figure 7-5. *Adding the Blueprint interface*

Once the Blueprint interface is added to the Blueprint actor, we are able to implement *interface events* that can be triggered from any other Blueprint, such as our VR pawn, where we connected it to the trigger event, so it will be fired off once an actor with an interaction interface is hit with the line trace and the trigger event. Our goal is to pick up items at the laser beam hit location, and move it around as long as the trigger button is pressed. Once we let go of the trigger button, the item is released at that location to drop down into the world and interact physically with the environment and other scene items. To accomplish that, we create an *event interaction* from the installed interface, connect it to the Attach To Component node, and set Simulate Physics to disabled. For the trigger release, we create an *event end interaction* from the same Interface and

connect it to the Detach From Actor node. It is important that we set the
Location/Rotation/Scale Rule Settings to Keep World, since we want to
interact at the hit location (see Figure 7-6).

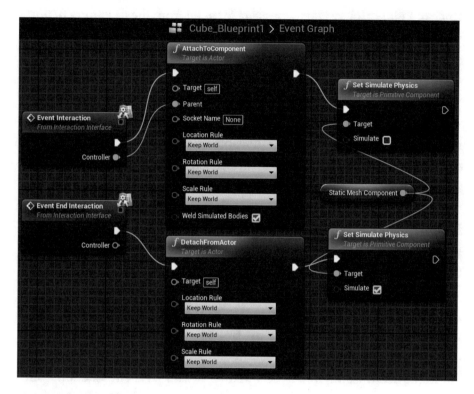

Figure 7-6. *Adding interface events*

We are now able to grab the cube with the laser beam, throw it in the
air and catch it again using the trigger button on our motion controller.

This example shows how useful Blueprint interfaces are to
communicate between Blueprints to activate events from one Blueprint to
the other.

Using the Blueprint Interface to Open a Drawer

Once the Blueprint interface message is called from the execution of our VR pawn's motion controller, we can implement the Blueprint interface event in any other Blueprint in our scene and execute whatever function we require for that specific scene object.

The next item that we will target with the interface call, is a drawer in a chest of drawers to be opened. Within our imported scene items, we have a chest of drawers with two movable drawers as separate objects. One of them will contain one of the keys we are searching for, as part of our gameplay. We will delete the second drawer, because it is easier to set up one Blueprint actor and then duplicate it. We are aiming to have two fully functional drawers that can be opened by selecting them with the laser beam and then using the trigger button to activate each one, which will result in the opening or closing movement.

To accomplish the desired functions, we need to convert the static mesh object to a Blueprint actor, and then install the Blueprint interface in the class settings of our Blueprint, by adding it in the Interfaces section under the Details tab.

In the event graph, we are now able to add the event interaction from our interaction interface. We connect it to a sequence node, which on the first position sets the actor's location in a vector variable named *location*. We restrict this sequencer branch with a *do once* node, because we only want this to happen the very first time. Without the *do once* node, the location would reset every time we trigger the event, which we don't want.

The second line of execution in the sequencer flip-flops the timeline, which means it opens it in case it is close and closes it in case it is open. The timeline is a simple two-second float track with automatic tangent interpolation, similar to the timeline we created in Chapter 4 (see Figures 4-42 and 4-43). The timeline drives the alpha between two vector lerp values, one with the original position that we set in our location variable and one with the location with an added value on the x axis. This value depends on the size of the drawer and the design of the chest of drawers that holds it. We will start with a value of 50 at first and then adjust it accordingly. The added value is inserted as a Vector Plus Vector node (see Figure 7-7).

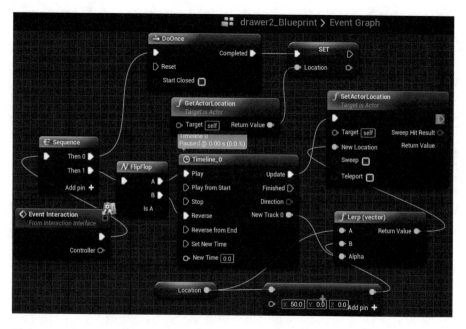

Figure 7-7. *Opening the drawer with an interface event*

After evaluating the drawers function and lerp settings, we can duplicate the Blueprint and position it in the other slot of the chest.

Now that the drawers are in place, we can position the first key in the lower drawer. To make it easier to pick up, we can position it on top of a small box inside of the drawer. To make sure the key and its box are moving with the drawer and to prepare it for further interaction, we convert the key's static mesh to a Blueprint actor and parent the Blueprint to the bottom drawer Blueprint by simply dragging it onto the drawer Blueprint inside of the world outliner. The key Blueprint is now slightly indented below the drawer Blueprint, which shows it is parented to it and will follow the movement of its parent.

Creating a Fixed Slot Inventory Interface

The next step is to make this level playable by creating a small inventory menu. As we have only three items to pick up, it is not necessary to create a dynamic system; instead, we will bind each item to a specific slot in the inventory interface.

In Chapter 6, we looked into creating UMG widget interaction menus in 3D space by placing in the environment. At the beginning of this project, we have already inserted the widget interaction component as a child of the motion controller component, including the Press Pointer Key interaction setup (in Figure 7-4). We will now add the corresponding widget component parented to the VR pawn's camera root, to interact with the inventory menu (see Figure 7-8).

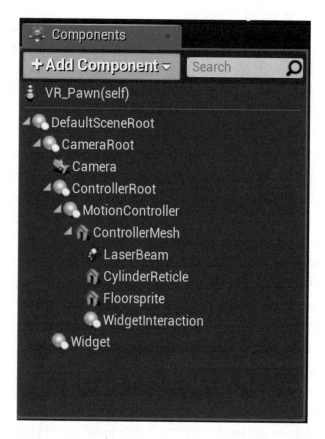

Figure 7-8. *Widget and widget interaction component for the inventory UMG*

Let us first describe what interactions are relevant to the inventory menu and then try to translate them into functioning Blueprints.

We want to call up the inventory with touch controller at any time in the game to review the items in it. If we activate a pickup item with our motion controller, we want the inventory to pop up and ask us if we want to add the item; the options are Add To Inventory and Close. If we add the item to the inventory, the item becomes Hidden In Game with Collision Disabled.

At the same time, an image of the item is displayed in the predefined slot in our inventory interface to show that it has become part of the inventory collection. If we activate an action item in the scene, which is an item that requires a pickup to perform an action, such as a lock that requires a key to unlock, the inventory menu pops up, as well, asking for a choice of inventory items to be used on the action item.

The item slots are interactive buttons, and if we select the wrong item for the action item, we receive the *Wrong item* message. If the correct item is picked and used, the inventory image is hidden; while the scene item's Hidden In Game and Disabled Collision settings are reversed at the new location and an action is performed. For example, the Blueprint will check if the other key is already activated, and if it is, will open the door.

The first two pickup items, the red key and the blue key, will be used in the first room on the red and blue lock next to the sliding door. The third pickup item, the orange bomb igniter, will be used in the second room near the exit to activate the bomb to blow off the door and kill the guard who is preventing us from exiting and finishing the game.

To create the UMG widget, we follow the same procedure as we did in Chapter 6. We right-click the content browser and select Widget Blueprint from the User Interface menu. We will call this widget VR UMG and give it a width of 200 and a height of 100. To make it visible in the viewport, we add a *border* container from the Designer palette, and give it a slight tint and scale it to the full size of the widget. This makes it easier to see it when positioning it.

After compiling and saving, we select the widget component in the VR pawn and add it into the Widget Class slot in the User Interface section of the Details panel. The VR pawn viewport allows us to arrange the widget, so it is position in front of the camera in a medium distance with a minor tilt.

The actual final position and tilt is a matter of personal preference and usability testing. It should be close enough to be easy to read without blocking too much of the view.

At Begin Play, the inventory menu widget should initially be hidden. By using the bottom touchpad of our motion controller, we should be able to toggle the visibility of the menu. To set that up in the event graph of the VR pawn, we connect the Motion Controller (R) Thumbstick Down input to a FlipFlop node. The FlipFlop node allows us to switch back and forth between the two visibility states.

We connect output A to a Hidden In Game node that is unchecked, which means visible, and a Set Collision enabled node. In output B, we set Hidden In Game to true, which means it will be invisible and collision is disabled. All nodes are targeting the widget component of the VR pawn that holds our widget class VR UMG (see Figure 7-9).

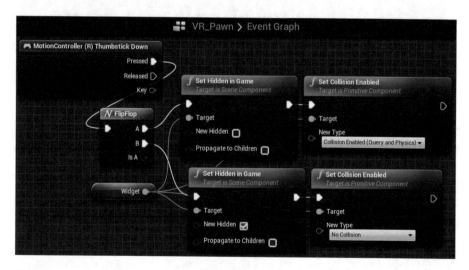

Figure 7-9. *Controlling the inventory menu with the touchpad down button*

Next, we need to set the initial hidden state by extending the line of execution from the event begin play that initialized the motion controller, as we set it up in Chapter 4. All we need to do is extend the execution to Set Hidden In Game with New Hidden checked, and Set Collision Enabled with New Type set to No Collision, referencing the Widget component in both node's targets (see Figure 7-10).

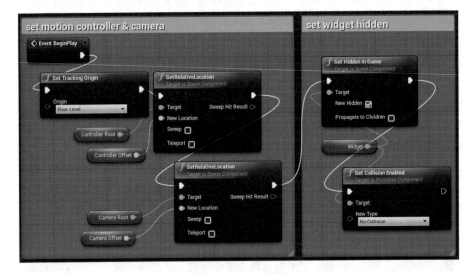

Figure 7-10. *Hiding the widget at begin play*

To interact with our motion controller's laser beam, we need to set the widget as a target for our trigger button, as we did in Chapter 6, by adding the press and release pointer key nodes to the trigger input event (seen in Figure 6-24).

We are now ready to create the content for our VR UMG widget. In the UMG designer, we drop three horizontal boxes on top of the border container that we set up. In the top position, we drop a text widget.

Next, in the bottom position, we drop a uniform grid with three buttons named Collect, Use, and Close. Finally, in the middle, we drop a uniform grid with three buttons that each holds an image of each pickup item that we rendered in Blender (see Figure 7-11).

Figure 7-11. *Building the UMG widget menu items*

Communicating with Casting and Event Dispatchers

To communicate between the inventory UMG widget and our VR pawn, we need to use a technique called casting. Casting establishes a line of communication between different Blueprint actors. A cast transforms a reference to a base object (a pawn for example) to a child/derived object (our VR pawn in this case) so that we can use its custom functions and properties.

The other feature to communicate across Blueprints is called an *event dispatcher*.

In Chapter 6, we used the Get All Actors Of Class node to target a specific Blueprint actor by triggering a UMG menu button, firing off a custom event in that Blueprint. In the next example, we use an alternative way to get the same result using an event dispatcher.

To set up the VR UMG, we to create an *event construct* and to use a Cast To node to cast to our VR pawn and set it as reference. This allows us to target the VR pawn in the UMG event graph, and we get access to the VR pawn's variables by getting or setting them.

217

In the VR UMG event graph, we select the close_button reference from the list of variables on the left. The variable is automatically created once a button is created. From the list of events at the very bottom, we select On Clicked, thus creating the on-clicked (close_button) event. To fire this button event across other Blueprints, we set up an event dispatcher by hitting the plus symbol in the Event Dispatcher section on the left panel below the Variables section. We give the newly created dispatcher the name Turn Off UI Dispatcher and compile. We are now able to create the corresponding node named Call Turn Off UI Dispatcher from the right-click menu. The small envelope icon on the node illustrates the fact that it will send out a message once triggered by the event (see Figure 7-12).

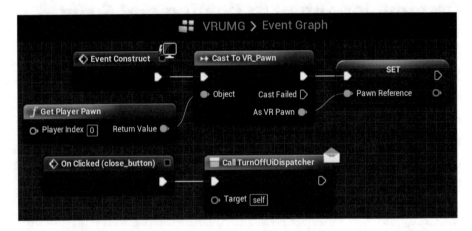

Figure 7-12. *Setting the VR pawn reference, and event dispatcher button call*

We will now set up the receiving side of the event dispatcher in the VR pawn event graph. Event dispatchers work in a way that a message is send out from the sender Blueprint and the receiving Blueprint has to listen by casting to the sender and by binding the executing event prior to it happening, by an event or tick. The binding can easily be done by extending the Event Begin Play execution (see Figure 7-10) which means the event binding is done at the very beginning and will after that be ready to be fired off once it receives the message from the sender.

Once we create the Cast To node referencing the widget component, we select Assign Turn Off UI Dispatcher from the right-click menu, and the required nodes are created for us. All we need to do next is connect the event to the respective widget visibility and collision nodes and setting them to turn off. The event dispatcher will then turn off visibility and collision for the VR pawn widget component when called from the menu button (see Figure 7-13).

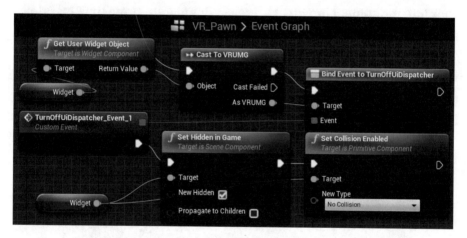

Figure 7-13. *Setting up the receiving end, of the Event Dispatcher*

We should now launch the compiled and saved project on the Oculus Go to verify that the button action works as expected.

Setting up and Binding Variables in the Widget Blueprint

In the next step, we need to set up variables and bind the ones that are affecting the interface display properties. We want to control these properties by casting from other Blueprints. The first variable will be based on an enumerator Blueprint that we need to set up. Enumerators are simple name lists that can later be used for switch nodes. We right-click into the content browser and select Enumerator from the Blueprint submenu. This creates a new enumerator Blueprint.

Under enumerators, in the opened Blueprint, we click the New button three times to create the new entries that we name according to our pickup items: red key, blue key, igniter. We save the enumerator named Collectibles (see Figure 7-14).

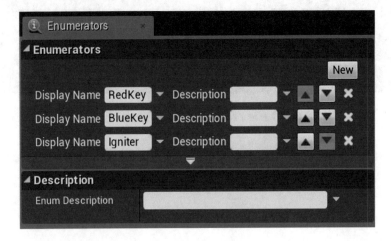

Figure 7-14. *Creating an enumerator list*

In the VR UMG widget Blueprint, we can now create a new variable under the Variables section on the left side of the event graph and name it collectible, for the variable type we set collectibles, referencing the enumerator that we just created.

The next variable that we need to create is of the type *text*, which we call *item text*. We want this variable to set the text in the text box that currently displays the word *Inventory* (as set up in Figure 7-11). To bind the variable to dynamically set the text for the text box, we select the text box item in the Widget Designer window Hierarchy tab and change the text property to Create Binding, under the Content tab in the Details panel on the right. By selecting our Item Text variable, we complete the binding (see Figure 7-15).

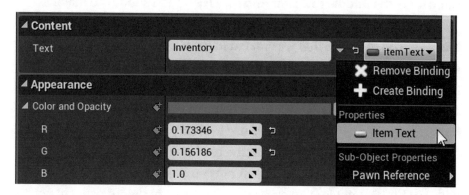

Figure 7-15. *Binding the text to a variable*

Next, we have to create three *boolean variables*. Booleans are basically on and off switches. The first one we call Red Key In Place; it allows us to check if the key has already been activated. The next two boolean variables are named Collect Button Active and Use Button Active. These two variables let us control whether the Collect and Use buttons are active. To control the button behavior, we need to bind them in the same way that created the binding for the item text. We select the button in the widget designer, and under Behavior in the Details panel, set the binding to the boolean variable that we created.

Setting up the Red Key Interaction

To pick up the red key, when the Blueprint actor is activated with the trigger button, we need to prepare the inventory menu and set the initial states of the Use and Collect buttons to Inactive and the items images to Not Visible in the Widget Designer Details panel.

Once the red key is activated by the motion controller's trigger button, we want the text on top to dynamically display *Collect Red Key?*. At the same time, the middle row slots and the Use button should be inactive.

To enable interaction with our red key Blueprint actor, we install the Blueprint interface that we created in the class settings in the same way we did for the drawer Blueprint (seen in Figure 7-5). After adding the Blueprint interface, we are ready to receive activation input once the Blueprint is selected by our VR pawn using the laser beam and trigger button. The added interface allows use to create an Event Interaction node that is ready to receive activation in the red key event graph.

Using the interface event, we can now build the Blueprint to interact with our VR UMG widget. At first, we need to cast to the VR pawn to enable visibility and collision for the inventory widget component that we added earlier with the Set Hidden In Game and Set Collision Enabled nodes.

The interface should now be open in front of the player. Now, we need to cast to the VR UMG to interact with the variables that were set earlier. The next item that we need to check is Red Key In Place. This variable is set to true if the key has already been collected earlier. In this case, we don't want anything to happen. If it is false, and the key has not already been collected, we want to set the item text on top of the inventory UI to *Collect Red Key?* by setting the Item Text variable.

Next, we want the Collect button to be active by setting the boolean variable to true and the Use button boolean variable to be set inactive. For the last step, we want to set the collectibles variable to be set to Red Key. This communicates to our VR UMG that we are currently interacting with the red key (see Figure 7-16).

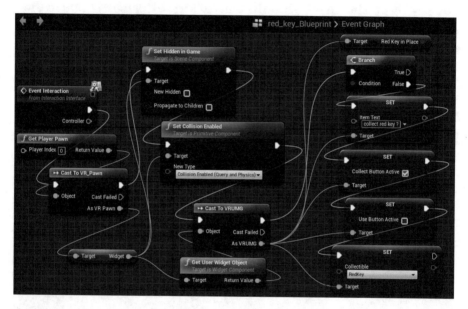

Figure 7-16. *Key and menu interaction*

Setting up the Collect Button

With the setup to this point, the user should be facing a menu with two choices: close the menu, which we already set up, or hit the Collect button to add the red key to the inventory.

When the user hits the Collect button with the motion controller laser and trigger button activation, we want the red key to disappear from the 3D environment and instead show up as an image in the designated item slot in the VR UMG inventory menu.

To accomplish that, we need to set up an event dispatcher named Hide Red Key Dispatcher in the VR UMG that calls the dispatched event in the red key Blueprint, to turn off visibility and collision. We do that in a similar fashion as before where the dispatched event's binding is done with the Event Begin Play node. We need to first cast to the VR pawn and then cast to the VR UMG because the widget is a component of the VR pawn. Once the dispatched event's binding is done, it will wait and listen for it to be called from the VR UMG (see Figure 7-17).

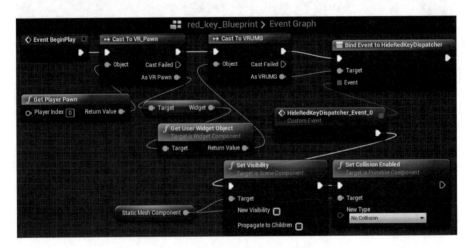

Figure 7-17. *The event dispatcher for the red key*

Next, we need to set up two more variables in the VR UMG Graph window. We set all item slots to Inactive and images to Not Visible, but we actually want to control these settings with variables. To do that, we need to create the variables that we can bind to these properties in the same way that we did previously. We create a boolean variable named Red Key Slot Active and bind it to the red key button slot's behavior under the Details panel in the Designer window, with the initial stage as Off.

For the image visibility, we create a variable of the eslate visibility type. *Eslate* refers to the Unreal slate system that the UMG system is based on. We bind the variable to the image with the initial state as set to Hidden.

We now have all components needed to fire off the Collect button. Whenever we create a UMG button, Unreal automatically creates a variable for it. All we need to do is select the Collect button from the variables list in the VR UMG Graph window, and then select the On Clicked event from the very bottom button event list. With the new Collect button event, we create a switch node based on our Collectibles variable. Since this variable was set to Red Key when it was fired off from the red key activation, the switch node will now read this value and set the switch to output accordingly to the Red Key out pin.

The Switch node is important as the Collect button will also be used for other items, so it needs to be set correctly to perform according to the requested activation item. Following the switch, we need to check again if the red key has already been collected by checking the Red Key In Place boolean variable. If it is set to true, nothing needs to happen, as the key is already collected. Only if the value is false, which means no red key has been collected prior, the execution continues. If so, we set the red key button slot to Active and the image to Visible, then we call the dispatcher to turn off the items visibility and collision in the 3D environment that we set up inside of the red keys event graph. Finally, we set the item text to display Red Key Collected and turn the Collect button to Inactive (see Figure 7-18).

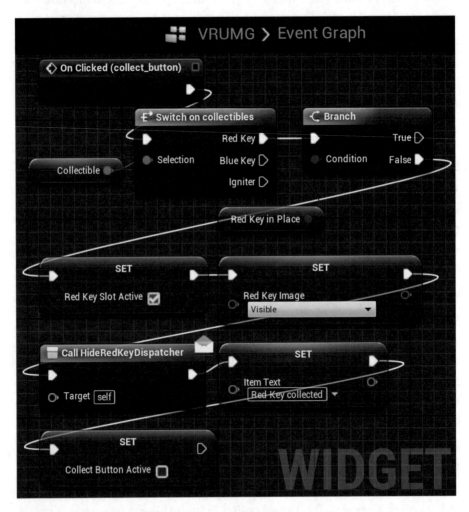

Figure 7-18. *Setting up the Collect button*

Setting up the Red Lock Interaction

After having set up the red key and collect interaction, we need to set up the Blueprint for the red lock action item interaction. When activating the red lock, which is next to the blue lock besides the closed door, we want the menu to pop up and ask us for a key. If there is nothing in our inventory, we can close the menu with the close button; however, if we picked up the red key earlier, we will want to use it.

To set up the VR UMG menu interaction, we convert the red lock static mesh into a Blueprint and add the Blueprint interface as we did for the other Blueprints under the class settings. Having done that, we can now receive input from the motion controller and trigger button. The red lock is a different category item from the collectibles, because it remains in position and expects to be activated with another item.

We will create another enumerator list Blueprint for the VR UMG graph in this category and call it Action Items. Just like in the previous enumeration list (as seen in Figure 7-14), we will list all the items in that category that need to be activated with inventory items, which are the red lock, the blue lock, and the bomb for the igniter. We now have everything needed to set up the interaction event for the red lock.

In the red lock Blueprint event graph, we create an *interaction event* from the interaction interface that we enabled earlier. From here, we cast to the VR pawn to set the VR UMG inventory menu to visible and collision enabled.

Following this, we cast to the VR UMG and check in a branch, as always, if the red key has already been applied. If true, nothing will happen; if false, we will set the item text variable to the message *Need Red Key*, the Collect button to Inactive, and the Use button to Active. Finally, we set the Action Item variable to Red Lock to communicate to the widget what item it is dealing with (see Figure 7-19).

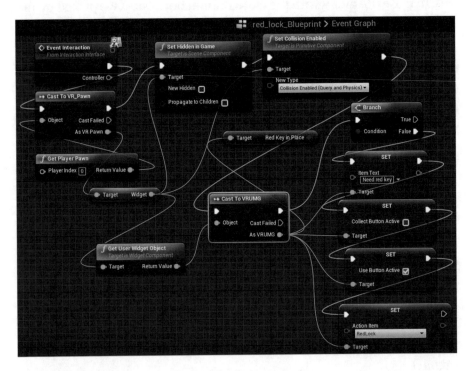

Figure 7-19. *Setting up the red lock interaction*

Selecting an Inventory Item

At this point, we are presented with an open inventory menu asking us to make a selection that can then be used. For the moment, we only have one item, the red key, but once all the other items are set up, it is very likely that we have more than one active item in our inventory. For that reason, we need to set up the inventory button slots to make a selection.

To set up the inventory slots, we have to make one more enumerator list Blueprint because we have yet another category of items, which are classified as items that are currently in the inventory. We set up the enumerator list, list the names (Red Key Inventory, Blue Key Inventory, and Igniter Inventory), and name the enumerator Inventory Items. Finally, we set up a button style, because we want the button to stay highlighted after making a selection, as the normal button behavior changes color only temporarily on hover or click interaction.

To set the button style permanently on a click event, we need to break the button style from a widget style referencing the red key button slot. The normal button style we will then break into the Slate Brush parameters that make up the design, change the slate color with a slate color input, and then put it back together by using the Make Slate Brush and Make Button Style nodes. To execute the button, we connect the red key button-slot click-event that was created from the button variable and the event list, to set an inventory item based on our Enumerator list, before setting the text to Inventory Red Key Selected, and finally setting the highlight button style that we defined earlier (see Figure 7-20).

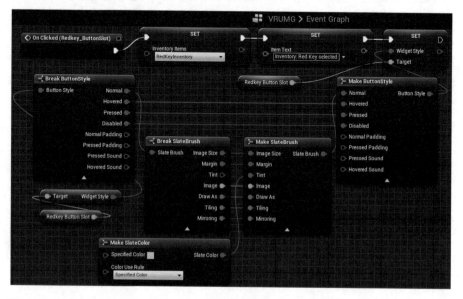

Figure 7-20. *Setting up the inventory slot selection button*

Setting up Use Button, Key, and Open Door Dispatcher

The last step in applying the key is setting up the Use button interaction, the Apply key, and the open door event dispatchers, plus one more boolean variable to check if a blue key has already been applied.

Once the Use button is activated, we want the key to appear in the lock position and turn around. If the other collectible key (the blue key that we will set up later) is applied, we want to open the sliding door.

If the blue key is not present, we will leave the red key in place and send a message to the VR UMG that the red key is in place. At the same time, we want the inventory menu to hide the red key inventory image, display the text *Key Applied*, set the Use button to inactive, and reset the widget style of the highlighted button back to normal. If the user selects an inventory slot other than that of the red key, we want the text to display *Wrong item*.

Let's first create the Apply Red Key Dispatcher in the VR UMG graph and then prepare the dispatch event in the red key event graph. Before setting it up, we need to find out where the key's final position and rotation will be. To do that, we temporarily copy the red key Blueprint and select Detach from the right-click menu to make sure it is not parented to the drawer anymore. We can now manually move and rotate the key into the desired lock position. Once in the correct location, we note down the transform values and delete the copy.

Inside of the red key Blueprint, we create two variables: target location and default rotation. We use these variables to store the copied location and rotation values for the final position and rotation of the applied red key.

With that in place, we extend the line of execution from the Begin Play Event that was used to bind the first event dispatcher. We bind the Apply Red Key Dispatcher Event the same way we did by casting to the VR pawn and then to the VR UMG.

The actual dispatcher that is listening to the Apply button in the VR UMG triggers, if executed, the following events: it sets visibility and collision for the key mesh as On, detaches itself from the drawer, and sets itself into the new target location and rotation at the lock. After half a second, it rotates around its x axis using a one-second float track in a timeline and a lerp rotate node between the initial position and the added 180 degrees on the x axis, to simulate a key being turned around (see Figure 7-21).

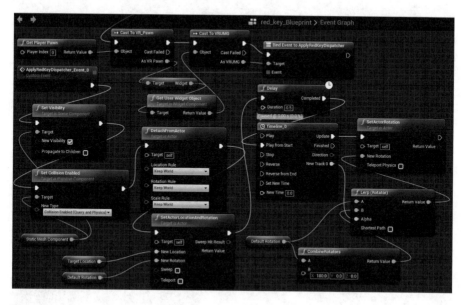

Figure 7-21. *Applying the key and turning it around*

After the key is turned around, the sliding door should open, but only if the blue key has also been applied, which we will check later with a boolean variable. If it has been applied and the door can open, we need to set up the door Blueprint in a similar way as the drawer Blueprint. In the VR UMG, we create a new event dispatcher called Open Door Dispatcher. We bind the dispatcher in the door Blueprint event graph with Begin Play by casting to the VR pawn and then to the VR UMG. The open door dispatcher that is listening to the VR UMG will set the location in a vector variable and lerp between the original position plus the width of the door offset by updating the actor location (see Figure 7-22).

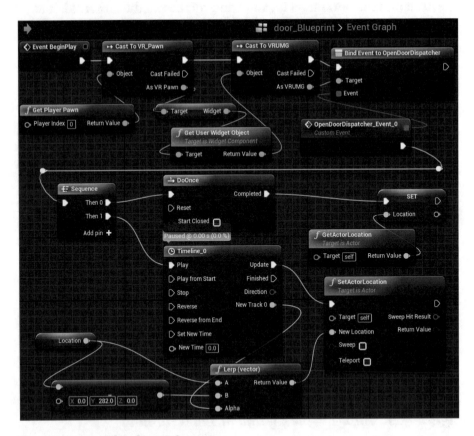

Figure 7-22. The door Blueprint

Having set up both dispatchers, we can now return to the VR UMG and set up the execution of the Use button. We select the Use button variable that was automatically created in the VR UMG Graph window and add the On Clicked event from the bottom-left list of events in the Details window.

Next, we add a switch node to get the value from the Action Item variable that was set when we activated the red lock. The red lock out pin of the switch, we connect to another switch to read the value of the inventory items variable that was set. If the user has the red lock activated and tries to apply the blue key inventory slot or the igniter inventory slot, he will get an error message: *Wrong item*.

If the red key inventory slot was correctly set, we continue the execution by hiding the inventory red key image and resetting the style of the button that was set to a highlighted orange background on selection. We can reset the button style by just borrowing from a neighboring button that hasn't been altered, in this case, the blue button slot.

After that, we set the Use button inactive and the red key slot inactive, and set the item text to Key Applied. From there, we call the Apply Red Key Dispatcher that set the key into the lock and rotates it, as was set up in the red key dispatcher earlier. The next node is a delay of two seconds, as we have to wait for the red key action to finish, plus an extra allowance to make it look more natural.

Finally, we need to set the variable Red Key In Place to True. We then check in a branch if the blue key has already been put in place. If set to True, it means both keys are in place, and the requirement to open the door is fulfilled and can be executed by calling the Open Door Dispatcher and displaying the item text *Success*. This will call the dispatcher that was set up to open the door. If the blue key is not present, nothing will happen.

We will later set up the blue key in a vice versa branch, where it checks the Red Key In Place variable that we just set, to verify if both keys are set in place to open the door (see Figure 7-23).

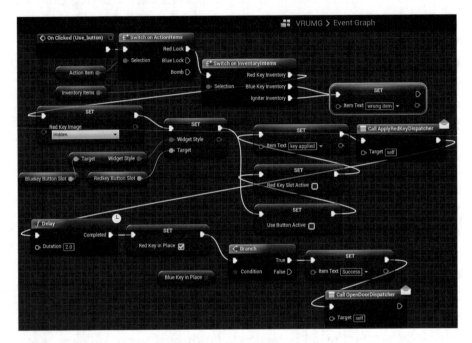

Figure 7-23. *Using the key to unlock the door*

We have now completed the setup for the red key and its lock, from picking it up, to selecting it in the inventory menu, to applying on the door to open it. Now we need to do the same for the blue key, the blue lock, the igniter, and the bomb. Only minor changes are required, such as changing the variable settings according to the items in use. For the blue key we don't need the Detach From Actor node, as it is not parented to the drawer. Instead, we want to hide it among a few boxes that need to be removed.

Setting up the Igniter and Bomb Dispatcher

The final position of the bomb and the igniter is set up in the second room near the exit. For the igniter we don't need any lerp movement in position when it is set to Use. Instead, we will add a delay after the igniter is placed in position by the Use button.

After the Use button trigger and delay have been completed, the event dispatcher triggers the bomb to blow off the exit door. We will bind the event dispatcher in the bomb Blueprint, that we created from the static mesh bomb, and spawn an emitter with a scale value of 10 at the actor location before destroying the actor. We use one of the explosion presets that come with the Unreal default content as the emitter. We select it from the emitter template pull-down in the emitter node (see Figure 7-24).

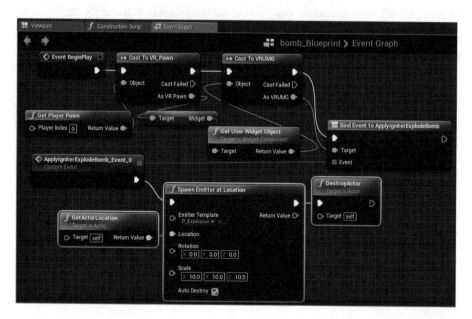

Figure 7-24. *Setting up the event dispatcher to explode the bomb*

On a side note, it should be mentioned that such visual effects as explosions are difficult to deal with in VR, due to the 2D nature of the particle sprites and also to the performance impact. Epic Games states in their VR best practice guide (`https://docs.unrealengine.com/en-us/Platforms/VR/ContentSetup`): "Some VFX tricks, like using SubUV Textures to simulate fire or smoke, do not hold up very well when viewed in VR. In many cases you are going to need to use static meshes instead of 2D particles to simulate VFX's like explosions or smoke trails."

Besides using static meshes for particles, there are numerous creative workarounds. For example, we could use the teleportation fade effect that was set up in Chapter 4 and switch it to white instead of black on a short timeline blast. In combination with sound and damage animation, this would look like a short intense explosion. Since our scene is fairly low poly, we can afford the explosion, and because the blast is extremely short, the sprites are not very obvious. We will review and validate this solution at the profiling stage.

The next trigger that we need to set up, is the animation to blow off the exit door. We will use Add Level Sequence under the Cinematics tab and add the transform keyframes for location and rotation (see Figure 7-25).

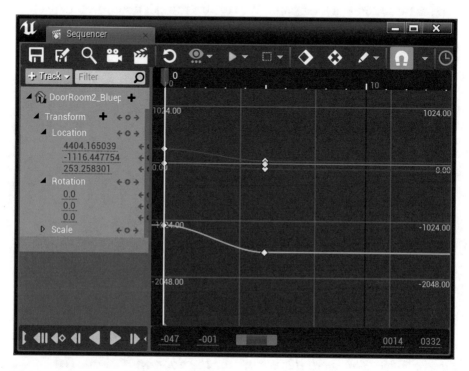

Figure 7-25. *The door animation*

It is important to select When Finished: Keep State under Animation Options in the right-click menu when selecting the sequencer track, to make sure the animation doesn't reset when finished.

Now we can set up the event dispatcher to trigger the sequence. The sequence could be played from anywhere in the scene, nevertheless we will set it up in the exit door Blueprint for the case that additional events need to be added at a later point. We convert the exit door to a Blueprint and bind the event dispatcher to the sequencer animation and a play node (see Figure 7-26).

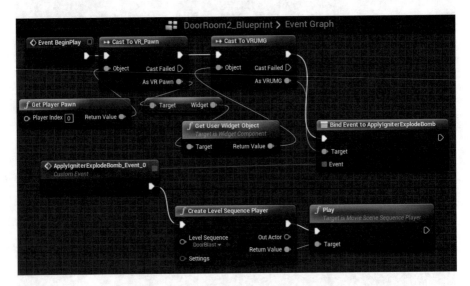

Figure 7-26. *The event dispatcher for the door animation. The explosion and the door animation will now trigger simultaneously*

Preparing the Guard Character

To prepare the character mesh for the Unreal animation system, we need to rig it with a skeleton. We could do the rigging manually with our third-party animation software, or use the popular Mixamo autorigger. Mixamo is an online system to rig characters and apply animation files, free of charge. The company has been acquired by Adobe, therefore a free Adobe user ID is required to login. After signing in, we can upload our character mesh, create a rig with the provided autorigging tools, and apply animations that can then be downloaded (see Figure 7-27).

Figure 7-27. *Applying animations in Mixamo*

We need three animation loops: idle, walking, and dying. We have to make sure that for the walk animation, the In Place checkbox is activated. Only with this setting will the animation be usable in the animation Blueprint. After reviewing and downloading all four files—the rigged character in T-pose and the three animation files—we can go into our animation software and make modifications to the animation.

We will use Akeytsu, an animation tool with a focus on game characters, which allows us to rig and animate characters by using an intuitive tool set including animation layers and Unreal skeleton presets. In our case, we want to make the walk cycle more pronounced and add an additional animation layer for the arm and hand animation to make it appear more aggressive. Akyetsu allows us to create new layer to the mixer where we can keyframe the additional skeleton action that is needed (see Figure 7-28).

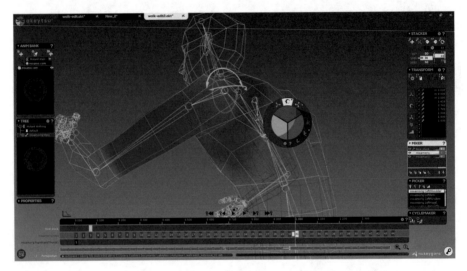

Figure 7-28. *Adding an animation layer in Akeytsu*

Once the animations are finalized and exported in the FBX format, we can import the files by drag and drop into the Unreal content folder. We will import the T-pose first and make sure that the Import option Skeletal Mesh is checked. In the next step, we will import the animation files. After importing the rig, *b-man* (as named in this example) should be available as a target skeleton (see Figure 7-29).

Figure 7-29. *Importing animations to target a skeleton*

Setting up the Character Animation Blueprint

Now we will create the animation Blueprint that is needed to control the character's walk and idle animation. By right-clicking in the content browser, we select Blendspace 1D from the Animation menu. Blendspace 1D allows us to blend between different animation files that we will later use to control how the character behaves according to input such as velocity. When setting up the Blendspace 1D Blueprint, we select our skeleton as the base when promoted, and drag the idle animation from the asset browser tab to the 0 position of the blendspace scale between 0 and 100. We place the WalkAttack animation at about 25, as we want the idle animation to transition to the WalkAttack animation at an early stage. To review the transition we can drag the green preview pin from left to right to get an idea of how it will look in the final setup (see Figure 7-30).

Figure 7-30. *Previewing the blendspace animation transition*

To control the blendspace transition by the character's speed velocity, we need to set up the animation Blueprint for it. We right-click into the content browser and select Animation Blueprint from the animation menu. We will call it Guard_ABlueprint. After opening the Blueprint we go to the animation tab next to the event graph and drag off Final Animation Pose to the left and select Add New State Machine from the right-click browser (see Figure 7-31).

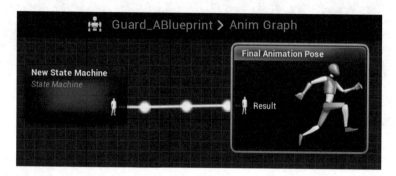

Figure 7-31. *Adding a state machine*

Once the state machine has been connected, we double-click it to open it and drag from the entry node to the right to create a new node called Idle Walk Attack (see Figure 7-32).

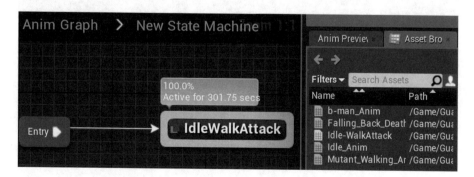

Figure 7-32. *Building the state machine*

We open the node that was just created by double-clicking and dragging the blendspace animation that was created next to the Final Animation Pose node. We connect the nodes and promote the speed input pin to a variable named Speed. We are now ready to receive speed input information to drive the animation (see Figure 7-33).

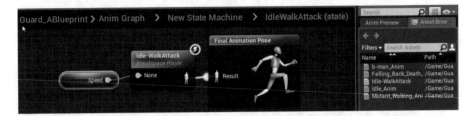

Figure 7-33. *The blendspace and speed variable driving the animation*

After compiling, we open the event graph. With the Blueprint Update Animation event, we set the speed variable by getting the velocity from the owning pawn with a vector length (see Figure 7-34).

Figure 7-34. *Controlling the animation speed by updating the speed variable*

Setting up the Character's Artificial Intelligence

We have successfully set up the blendspace and animation Blueprint to drive the character's animation behavior when moving forward, but we have not yet determined under what rules the character will move to any location. We will do that by setting up the required Blueprints, which are AI Controller, Behavior Tree, and Blackboard. We create the AI Controller by searching for it in the right-click menu and naming it Guard_AIController. We create the Behavior Tree and Blackboard from the right-click menu under Artificial Intelligence and name them Guard_BT And Guard_ Blackboard.

After opening the blackboard, we create a new entry in the Blackboard key list, name it Move Location, and select the type as Vector in the Details panel.

Blackboard keys are values that can communicate with variables for other behavior tree components such as *tasks*. We open the behavior tree and add a new task Blueprint from the Behavior Tree toolbar. This creates a new Blueprint in our content browser, which we can rename and thus call it BTTask_FindLocation. We open the task Blueprint and add a Receive Execute AI event, cast it to the VR pawn, get the VR pawn's location, and set the location value to a variable of the type Set Blackboard Value As Vector, which we name Move Key. The last node is Finish Execute with Success checked as true. This ensures that the behavior tree can execute and move on to the next task (see Figure 7-35).

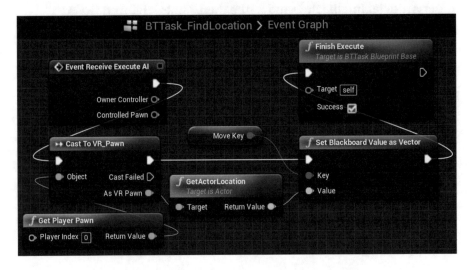

Figure 7-35. *Setting the task to get the pawn's location*

We can now open the behavior tree and drag off a Selector node. From the Selector node, we drag off a Sequencer node, which gives us the option to select a task. In the Details panel, we set Move Key to the Blackboard Move Location variable. We then drag off a Move To task from the sequencer and make sure that the Blackboard Key: Move Location is selected in the Details panel (see Figure 7-36).

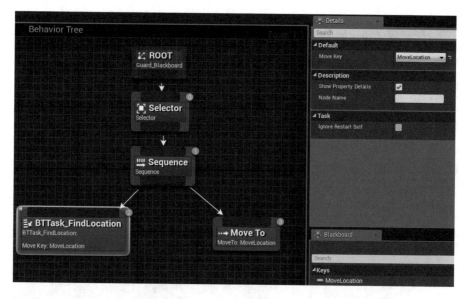

Figure 7-36. *Creating the behavior tree*

The way we set up the behavior tree, it will pass through the selector and execute the sequencer from left to right, at first finding and setting the VR pawn's location and then moving toward it.

The AI that our behavior tree generates requires a *nav mesh*, which we have already set up. Once in place, it actively resolves complex pathfinding around obstacles.

Setting up the Guard Character Blueprint

We can now create the character Blueprint for our guard character by right-clicking into the content browser, selecting Blueprint Class, and from Parent Classes, select Character Blueprint. The character Blueprint inherits from the pawn Blueprint but comes with additional features, such as complex character movement controls. We name our character Guard Character BP, open it, and select the mesh component. From the Skeletal Mesh drop-down menu, we select our imported character base, and from the Animation class above it, we select the Guard_ABlueprint animation Blueprint that we created earlier (see Figure 7-37).

Figure 7-37. *Setting skeletal mesh and animation class for the guard*

Finally, we select the base component Guard Character BP (Self) in the Components window. In the Details panel, we select the Guard AIController Blueprint from the AI Controller Class drop-down menu in the Pawn section (see Figure 7-38).

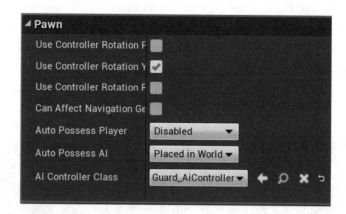

***Figure 7-38.** Setting the AI controller*

For our character to access the behavior tree logic, we open the AI Controller Blueprint named Guard_AIController that we created earlier and create an On Possess event in the event graph, which casts to the Guard Character BP to run the behavior tree, where we set the BT Asset to the behavior tree that we created named Guard_BT (see Figure 7-39).

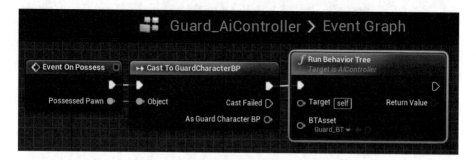

***Figure 7-39.** Setting the AI controller to run the behavior tree*

In the last step of the character setup, we want to tie the guard character into the explosion event. When the bomb goes off, we want the guard to play the death animation that we imported and then remain dead on the floor. To do that, we bind the Apply Igniter Explode Bomb Event Dispatcher to the Begin Play event as we did with the bomb and the door animation, by casting it to the VR pawn and VR UMG. We use the custom event to play the *Falling Back Death* animation that we imported targeting our character mesh. Finally, we unpossess the controller; otherwise, the AI would continue to follow the VR pawn as a moving corpse on the floor (see Figure 7-40).

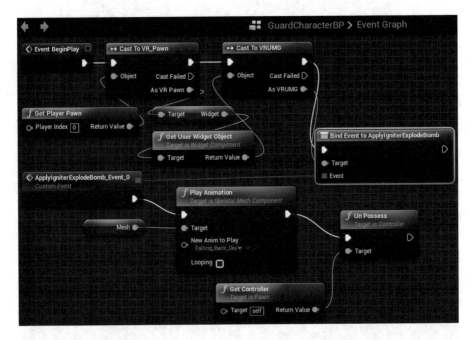

Figure 7-40. *Setting up the death trigger*

Testing the scene on the Oculus Go will have the guard character follow us around and coming straight at us after we have entered the second room.

Creating a Health System

We want to show a health bar when we enter the second room and to collect health pickups. When the guard character comes close to us, we receive health damage. When health drops below zero, we die, and the level restarts. To create a health bar, we create a float variable in the VR pawn with the default value of 0.2 and make it public. Using the Widget Blueprint, we create another UMG widget and call it Health UMG. In a horizontal box, we create two vertical boxes: one with the text health and one with the progress bar (see Figure 7-41).

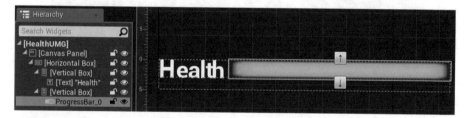

Figure 7-41. *Setting up the health bar*

In the UMG's Event Graph editor, we set up an event construct node, cast to the VR pawn, and promote the VR pawn to variable as we did in the previous UMG. This allows us to access the health variable that was created earlier (see Figure 7-42).

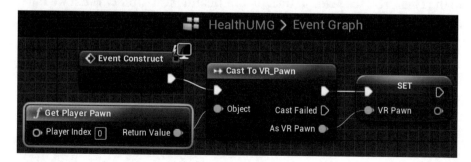

Figure 7-42. *Casting to the VR pawn*

We can now bind the VR pawn's health variable to the percentage of the progress bar in the UMG (see Figure 7-43).

Figure 7-43. *Binding the progress to the health variable*

Back in the VR pawn, we create another widget component in the size of the UMG and parent it to the VR pawn camera. This ensures the health bar is locked to the head movement. By testing on the Oculus Go, we adjust the positioning to a comfortable spot on the upper left-hand side. To control the visibility of the health bar, we create a Blueprint named Health Space containing only a collision box in the size of the second room.

Back in the VR pawn, we create a capsule component, to make sure we have a collidable object and create a begin and end overlap event that casts to the Health Space actor to turn on our health bar visibility when we enter the second room and turn it off when we exit it (see Figure 7-44).

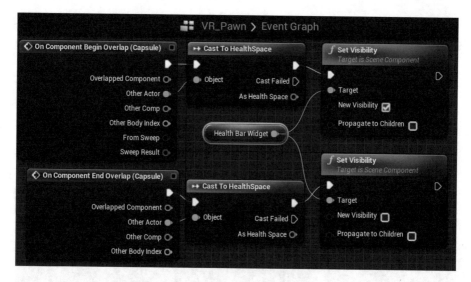

Figure 7-44. Controlling the health bar visibility

Creating the Health Pickups

To set up our health pickups, we convert the green cross static mesh that was imported in the beginning to a Blueprint and add the Blueprint interface under the class settings as we did with the other scene actors.

Next, we create an interface event that casts to VR pawn, setting the health with an additional 0.1 float value before it is destroyed (see Figure 7-45).

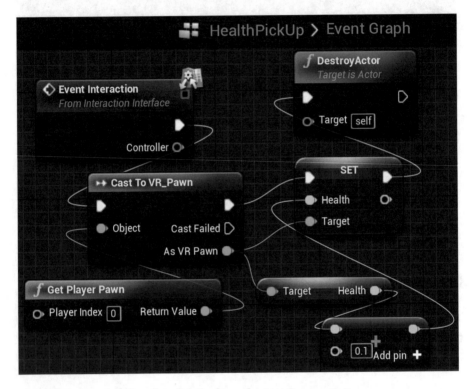

Figure 7-45. *Adding health before destroying actor*

Before duplicating the actor in the scene, we add a rotating component under the component tab. A rotating component is a convenient way to have a pickup continuously rotate to attract attention. In the default settings, it rotates 180 degrees per second around the z axis, which is usable for our situation.

Once we place the actor in the scene, we can duplicate it eight times. As the default health is 0.2, adding 0.1 eight times brings the health to 100% in the range between 0 and 1. In our situation, it is convenient that the maximum cannot exceed 1, so we don't have to clamp the range.

We can now test the scene using the motion controller. Pointing the laser beam and hitting the trigger button destroys the pickup and add the extra amount of health as expected (see Figure 7-46).

Figure 7-46. *Rotating health pickups*

Creating Health Damage

We want the AI-driven guard character to damage the VR pawn's health, once it gets into close proximity. To receive damage we add a collision capsule component to the VR pawn. We will start out the game with the low health value of 0.2. The guard character will do 0.3 damage once it comes near, which means we have to pick up health boosters to survive the encounter and get to the bomb to initiate the igniter to blow off the exit door, before our health is attacked too many times. If our health goes below zero, we die and the game starts over. To cause damage, we will create an extra-large collision box on our guard character and call it Damage Collision (see Figure 7-47).

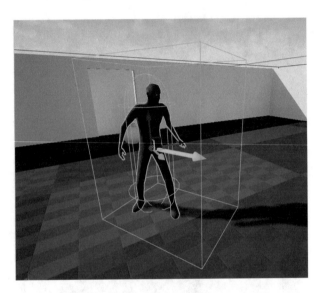

Figure 7-47. *Character with damage collision box*

Inside the guard character event graph, we create an Overlap event on the Damage Collision box, cast it to the VR pawn, and subtract 0.3 from the character's health variable, if the value is above 0 as set per branch condition. If the value falls below 0, we will get the current level name and open it, which basically means we die and respawn by restarting the level (see Figure 7-48).

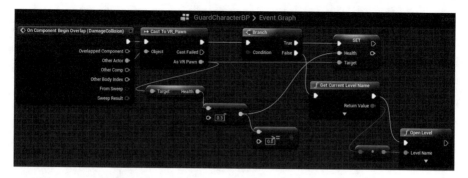

Figure 7-48. *Creating damage and death*

Refinements

Our game system is now complete. We created the base conditions for a functional game. In the next possible steps, we could fine-tune its mechanics.

The to-do list is as follows. Create conditions that action items can only be activated in close proximity. Add color and sound effects to pick up and action items. Use custom background images and designs for the inventory menu. Add additional animation states for the guard AI-character. The list is open ended. Once everything is refined, we can replace the stand-in objects with textured custom geometry to finalize the look and feel.

Conclusion

We created a small puzzle game with two keys to unlock a door and an igniter to equip a bomb. Using a fixed slot inventory menu helped us to manage the puzzle items. We created an AI-driven opponent to damage our health in the second room. To recover our health, we set up a number of rotating pickups. The health pickups helped us to reach the exit to finally deploy the bomb, blow off the exit door with an explosion, and kill the guard AI-character.

During this project, we used casting, Blueprint interfaces, and event dispatchers to communicate between the different Blueprint actors. All interactions were handled by our motion controller, including its trigger button to fire off events. Locomotion was managed through the flexible locomotion set up in Chapter 4. This chapter demonstrates how to use the flexible different Blueprint communication systems in a mobile VR project targeted at the Oculus Go.

CHAPTER 8

Performance, Profiling, and Optimizations

Introduction

In this chapter, we look at the various profiling and optimization tools that are available in the Unreal editor and when testing on the Android target platform. It is usually a good idea to start profiling early and have an eye on the frames per second (fps) at any stage of development to eliminate roadblocks when they occur.

It is advisable to develop a high awareness of what the typical VR performance killers are and try to avoid them, or work around them using best practices guides and creative ideas. If we come across a stubborn performance bottleneck, we will use our profiling toolset to identify the exact nature of the bottleneck to then be able to eliminate it. We do that by looking for spikes and excessive numbers in our CPU and GPU profiling reports. Once identified. we can redesign, rearrange, reduce, or eliminate the specific elements or events causing the trouble.

© Cornel Hillmann 2019
C. Hillmann, *Unreal for Mobile and Standalone VR*,
https://doi.org/10.1007/978-1-4842-4360-2_8

Developing an Optimization and Profiling Strategy

During the course of this chapter, we will develop a strategy to optimize assets and projects setup when building the scene and create a roadmap to address bottlenecks in the later stages through profiling and optimization tools. Optimization plays a major role in mobile and standalone VR. VR graphics are on the cutting edge of what is possible on Android-based mobile platforms. The richer and more complex the content, the greater the effort that has to be put into content optimization to squeeze the full performance potential out of the platform and run a VR project at a minimum of 60 fps.

When Oculus CTO and optimization guru John Carmack told an audience of VR developers to "embrace the grind," he meant the hard work it takes to make things work within the limitations of mobile GPUs and CPUs.

Due to the performance challenges, it has become standard that even small-to-midsize teams have positions for full-time profiling and performance engineers. While that is certainly the best possible scenario, we are approaching the issues from a different angle. We will tackle the tasks from the perspective of the VR ninja and CG generalist. What this means is, we will not be planning to be full-time profiling and performance engineers; instead, we will take full advantage of the available toolset, follow best-practice guidelines, and be aware of the problem areas and issues to avoid.

Our strategy is to target the most common areas sensitive to mobile VR performance and to find workarounds at the early stages of developing our content. In the later stages, we will use the different tools in Unreal and Oculus to analyze and profile GPU and CPU activity, and measure it against our target expectations. Doing that, we will close in on bottlenecks and dissect the rendering pipeline to isolate the problems using third-party analytic tools.

Early Planning

Within the early stages of scene building and asset creation, we can easily pay attention to the most basic rules for mobile VR, which comes down to not having too much going on at the same time. Too many objects and too many textures will result in an overkill of draw calls and kill our target frame rate. Our target baseline is the minimum requirement for the Oculus store, which is 60 fps minimum, 50–100 draw calls per frame, and 50,000–100,000 triangles or vertices per frame.

When developing concepts, we should keep in mind how we can break the design down into reusable modules, to make the scene more efficient. The larger the VR scene is, the more important it becomes to use modular design elements. Modular design typically follows a fixed grid pattern, so that the modular set pieces can be combined in different variations as instances during level design. To make repeating assets less obvious, the scene is typically broken up by props and decals. A good practice is to study well-done modular design pieces that are available for free; for example, in the Unreal marketplace (see Figure 8-1).

Figure 8-1. *Working with modular assets from the Unreal marketplace*

When creating assets with PBR textures, we should always consider baking the PBR channels into one color map. That means taking a snapshot of the lighting situation and burning that into the combined color map. Normalness, metalness, and roughness, including any reflections and ambient occlusion, are permanently projected to the color map, which means that the material will not interact with the scene light, environment reflection, or the viewing angle anymore. Nevertheless, it is very often a good way to add visual complexity to the scene while managing the performance hit.

Substance Painter has an excellent solution for baking PBR maps by using the Baked Lighting filter. When dropped into the Layer window, it automatically creates a new material called *baked lighting*. The filter settings allows fine-tuning the environment input, including lights, and the PBR material parameters in the color map (see Figure 8-2).

Figure 8-2. *Baking PBR channels into a color map in Substance Painter*

Substance Painter allows you to preview the baked result using the Base Color viewport setting. Once exported as a single RGB map, it can be used in an Unreal base color material slot using an unlit shading model.

Using Blurry Blob Shadows Instead of Dynamic Shadows

In Chapter 6, we talked about the importance of keeping all lights as static lights to fully bake the scene's shadows into the lightmap. One of the worst offenders when it comes to mobile- and standalone-VR performance are dynamic lights and shadows. Dynamic lights and shadows have a dramatic impact on performance. In almost all cases, the performance cost is way too high to be justifiable. The fact is that mobile GPUs have in general very tight bandwidth constraints and any render-to-texture effects, including dynamic lights and shadows, or any kind of post-processing effects are a waste of valuable bandwidth.

For that reason, it is important to use only static lights without any dynamic shadows wherever possible. This allows us to fully bake the lighting results, in order to manage performance. However, if we have moving objects in our scene, we have to assess how important the shadow would be. In some cases, it would be no problem to completely do without shadows, such as a high-flying object, or in cases where the viewing angle deems them unnecessary. Nevertheless, typical scene actors that need shadows to look convincing are characters, creatures, and vehicles with floor contact or floor proximity.

For cases in which a shadow is important for the overall scene aesthetics, we can consider an old-school technique called blurry blob shadow.

Blob shadows go back to the early days of gaming in the 1990s. It was used in games such as *Quake* to simulate a blurry ground shadow without costing much performance.

To create a blob shadow, we create a cube that intersects with the floor under the character and assign a blob shadow material. The blob shadow cube is parented to the character so that it follows the actor around. To create the blob shadow material, we set Blend Mode to Translucent and

Shading to Unlit in the Materials attributes. The material is based on the World Position Behind Translucency node, which we subtract from the object position input data, before we pipe it into a sphere mask multiplied by 0.5 and connect it with the opacity channel. The shadow color input determines what tint we want to give the shadow and the sphere mask radius setting determines the softness of the shadow result (see Figure 8-3).

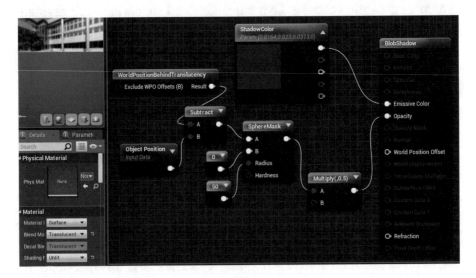

Figure 8-3. Setting up a blob shadow

In our example, the radius is set to 50 to give a result with soft and blurry edges. Once we drop the material on to the cube that is intersecting with the floor, the shading result only shows up on the intersecting area (see Figure 8-4).

Figure 8-4. *Testing the blob shadow on a parented cube*

If we want a rectangular-shaped shadow, we can replace the sphere mask node with a box mask 2D node (see Figure 8-5).

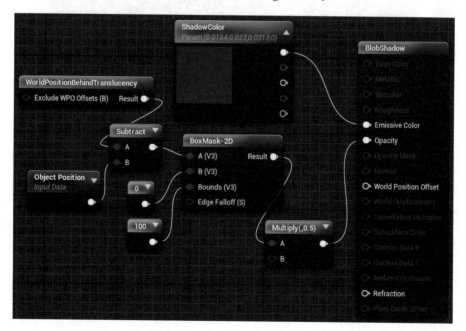

Figure 8-5. *Creating a rectangular shadow material*

In our rectangular shadow example, the edges are left sharp. To test how the shadow not only interacts with the floor but also with other scene objects, we can move the parent around the scene and evaluate how the shadow of the child cube interacts with other intersecting surfaces (see Figure 8-6).

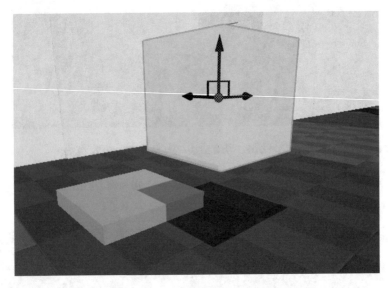

Figure 8-6. *Testing the rectangular shadow material*

Next to this method, there are a number of other techniques, such as using circle decals on the floor, or if more realism is required, complex setups that involve shadow-sprites that are linked to the player's skeleton bones. These kinds of setups can get very elaborate and very often require a good amount of math operations to produce convincing results, which could result in a heavier CPU load. In most cases, a simple blurry blob shadow will do the job.

Optimizing Texture Size

When creating textures, we very often want to be on the safe side and create textures that are large enough for any situation, including a high-res, close-up placement. But it also happens more than often that after designing the level, the actual use of the textured object ends up scaled down in the background. For that reason, it is important to assess at what size the texture is actually used at any time in the game. For example, in the flexible teleportation setup that we used in Chapters 4, 6, and 7, we imported a PNG floor sprite that was created in a vector program. We can check how this texture is actually used inside of the game by opening the Texture Stats page in the Statistics window from the main menu (see Figure 8-7).

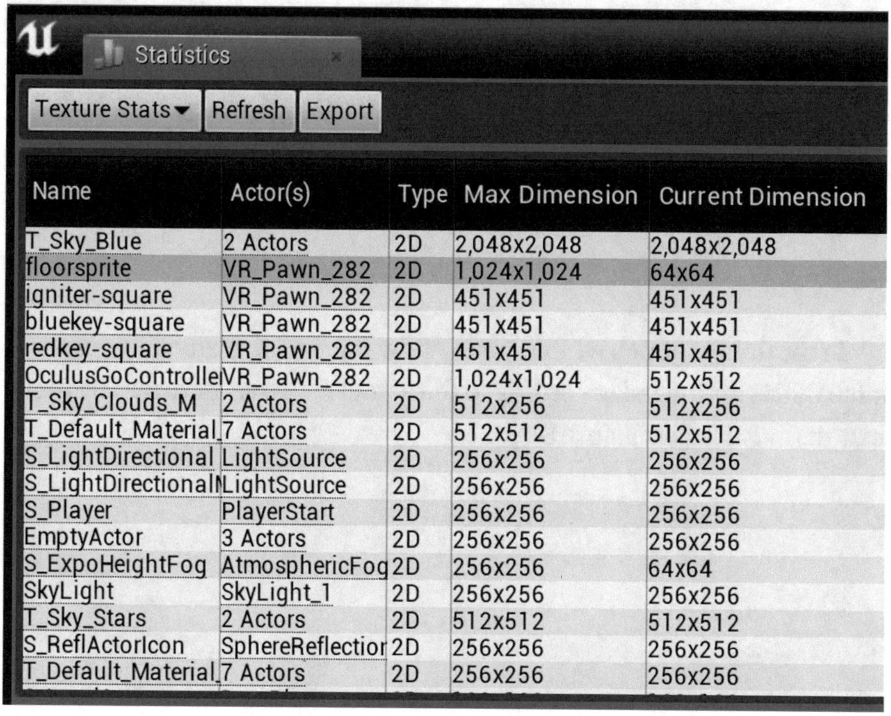

Name	Actor(s)	Type	Max Dimension	Current Dimension
T_Sky_Blue	2 Actors	2D	2,048x2,048	2,048x2,048
floorsprite	VR_Pawn_282	2D	1,024x1,024	64x64
igniter-square	VR_Pawn_282	2D	451x451	451x451
bluekey-square	VR_Pawn_282	2D	451x451	451x451
redkey-square	VR_Pawn_282	2D	451x451	451x451
OculusGoControlle	VR_Pawn_282	2D	1,024x1,024	512x512
T_Sky_Clouds_M	2 Actors	2D	512x256	512x256
T_Default_Material	7 Actors	2D	512x512	512x512
S_LightDirectional	LightSource	2D	256x256	256x256
S_LightDirectional	LightSource	2D	256x256	256x256
S_Player	PlayerStart	2D	256x256	256x256
EmptyActor	3 Actors	2D	256x256	256x256
S_ExpoHeightFog	AtmosphericFog	2D	256x256	64x64
SkyLight	SkyLight_1	2D	256x256	256x256
T_Sky_Stars	2 Actors	2D	512x512	512x512
S_ReflActorIcon	SphereReflection	2D	256x256	256x256
T_Default_Material	7 Actors	2D	256x256	256x256

Figure 8-7. *Checking the texture statistics*

Here, we can get an overview on how our textures are currently used in the game. We notice that the floor sprite texture has a max dimension much larger than is needed for the current Dimension tab. This means inefficient texture management and increased load times. We can fix that by opening the Texture Properties editor and reviewing the Compression settings (see Figure 8-8).

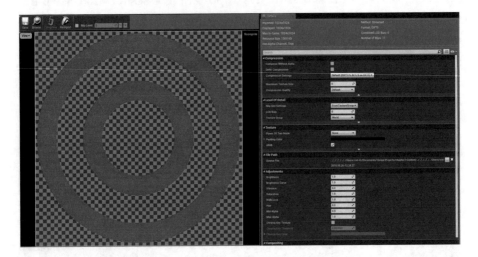

Figure 8-8. *Optimizing the floor sprite reticle*

In the details panel, we can now set the maximum texture size to a value that is optimized according to the actual usage as indicated by the texture statistics (see Figure 8-9).

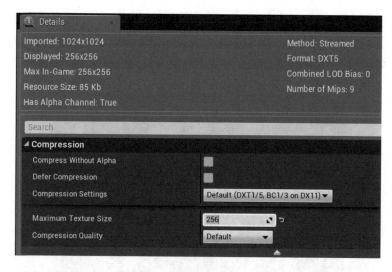

Figure 8-9. *Resetting the texture size in the compression settings*

Then, checking the texture statistics, we should also make sure that they are in a power of two (64×64, 128×128, 256×256, 512×512, 1024×1024, etc.), unless they are UMG UI elements and set as User Interface 2D (RGBA) in the compression settings.

VR Rendering Tab Settings

The Rendering section of the project settings has a number of performance relevant checkboxes.

First, mobile MSAA in the Mobile section should be set to 2 × MSAA or 4 × MSAA to improve anti-aliasing. In the VR tab, Mobile Multi-View and Mobile Multi-View Direct have to be checked because they make stereo rendering much more performance efficient. It is important to verify ES3.1 against the targeted hardware because some older Samsung phones only support ES2.

Monoscopic Far Field is a helpful feature for distant scene objects, that don't benefit from stereoscopic eye separation. Enabling Monoscopic Far Field allows us to tag distant scene object as monoscopic and adjust the mono culling distance in the world settings, reducing the load on the rendering pipeline. To make the stat overlay readable, Debug Canvas In Layer should be enabled when profiling on the headset (see Figure 8-10).

Figure 8-10. *VR render settings for optimization*

We should also double-check that HDR has been turned off in the Mobile section.

Baking Far Distant Environments to a Skybox

If a scene is too overloaded with far-distance objects, we can consider baking these background scene items into an image skybox.

To capture scene elements that are in the far distance, we hide the close-up objects temporarily and use Unreal's Scene Capture Cube. The scene capture cube has the appearance of a camera and has to be dropped into the scene and positioned accordingly. In the Details panel under the

Scene Capture section, we select Cube Render Target under Create New Asset from the pop-up menu, in the Texture Target section of the Scene Capture tab (see Figure 8-11).

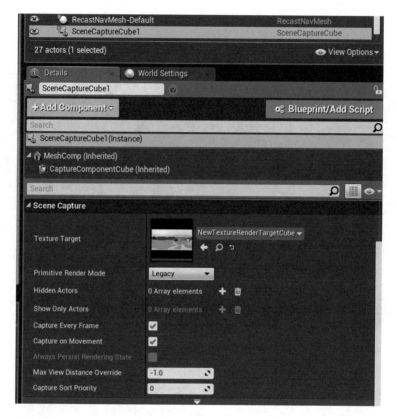

Figure 8-11. *Capturing the distant environment*

First save and then open the new texture render target cube asset that was created. We can set the resolution to 2048 in the Size x field. After saving, we can now right-click the asset and select Create Static Texture. This creates a permanent copy with our required resolution that we can use for our skybox. Using the new skybox texture, we can now create the material by using a constant three-vector set at zero, connected to a reflection vector WS node and texture sample parameter cube, as an emissive color input to our new sky material, set to unlit and two-sided in the material settings. As the last step, we select our new render cube texture in Material Expression Texture Base and uncheck Automatic View Mip Bias (see Figure 8-12).

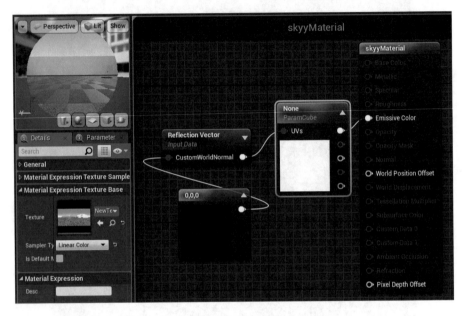

Figure 8-12. *Setting up the skybox material*

If we already have a sky sphere in our scene, we can edit it to add our new skybox material with the scene capture material; otherwise, we just add a new sky sphere from the Unreal editor into the scene. We just have to do some minor changes to the construction script of the sky sphere Blueprint. Construction scripts are always executed at initialization. In our example, it sets up the sphere mesh and its material.

In the Construction Script editor, we select our sky material under the Source Material drop-down menu of the Create Dynamic Material Instance node. Anything that comes after this node can be deleted or disconnected. Once compiled, we should see our captured environment as the scene background (see Figure 8-13).

Figure 8-13. *Updating the Sky Sphere Blueprint*

The sky sphere with our screen capture is monoscopic. There would be no point in rendering it as stereoscopic as long as the minimum distance of the captured environment objects is at least 20 meters from the user's camera. At around 20 meters distance from VR camera, the depth perception tapers off. The maximum perceivable depth means that scene object beyond that distance can be considered for a skybox capture to offload distant objects and reduce scene complexity.

Level of Detail

Unreal offers a convenient level of detail (LOD) system that should be used aggressively with large VR scenes and highly detailed meshes. To set it up, we open the mesh in the Static Mesh editor and select one of the presets from the LOD group, in LOD settings as a starting point. Once we select Large Prob from the presets, four LOD levels are automatically created for us. We can now test how the LOD meshes get swapped out according

to the camera distance by using the Level of Detail Colorization ➤ Mesh
LODs View mode. To edit and customize the autogenerated distances, we
can uncheck Auto Compute LOD Distances and set new values for the new
breakpoint using the screen size as a reference (see Figure 8-14).

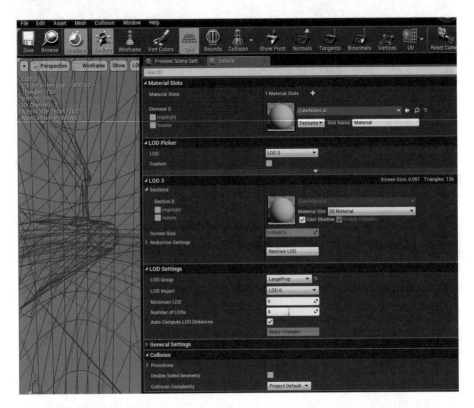

Figure 8-14. *Setting up LODs*

Identifying Problems Using Optimization Viewports

Some of the worst offenders when it comes to VR performance are foliage
and particles, or anything relying heavily on translucency. For that reason,
it is a good idea to avoid them altogether, whenever possible, unless it is a
short blast with reduced and optimized sprites.

A small test confirms the heavy performance load, for example, if we put a number of fires and smoke emitters into a VR scene. The spawning sprites from the emitter will wear the headset down, bringing down frame rates and increasing the thermal load, resulting in increased temperature.

Unreal comes with a helpful set of optimization viewports that help to identify the problem areas. The most important one of these optimization viewports is the shader complexity viewport. Changing the default Lit view mode in the Viewport menu to shader complexity under optimization view modes will give a visual indication on a color scale those areas that are most demanding, indicating per-pixel complexity of shaders that are executed. If we zoom in on our example using a fire and smoke emitter from the engine content, we can see by the red color how demanding the rendering is for the overlapping particle sprites (see Figure 8-15).

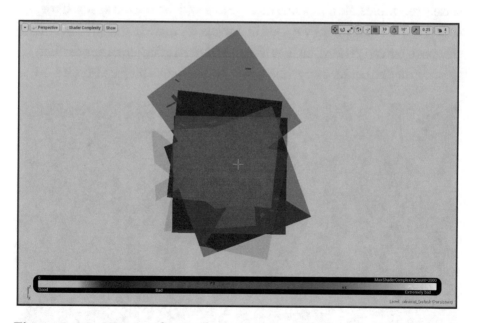

Figure 8-15. *Viewing fire and smoke using the shader complexity view mode*

We should check our project with this viewport on a frequent basis to make sure we don't have any serious showstoppers hidden in the scene.

While shader complexity is one of the most important optimization viewports, we should also look at the other options that are most helpful in optimizing a VR scene.

The quad overdraw viewport mode is important for detecting problems when it comes to overlapping transparent space, as this is also common in foliage and particles. When using alpha textures for transparency, we have to take into consideration that alpha planes use alpha testing, which means it requires an additional draw call.

The best workaround is to keep the alpha mapped polygon as close to the shape it represents as possible, to reduce the amount of fully-transparent pixels on screen. This can be done by cutting a polygon shape that most closely resembles the alpha mask shape to avoid the wasted space. If we review the fire and smoke we used in our last example in the quad overdraw viewport, we can clearly see how the most overlapping alpha sprites that spawn from the center carry the highest performance hit (see Figure 8-16).

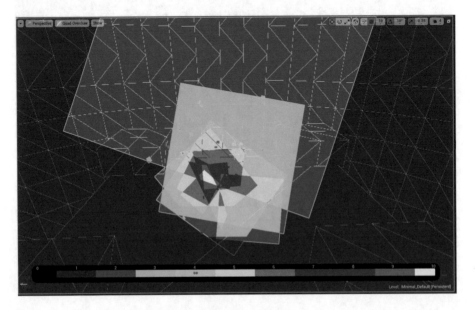

Figure 8-16. *The cost of overlapping alphas*

The next viewport mode to consider is the lightmap density view mode. Lightmap density shows the texel density of a scene per object. Usually, we tweak the lightmap resolution settings visually until the shadow quality that is baked into the lightmaps is satisfying. However, the fact is that light maps are actually stored textures, so we have to make sure that there is no excessive and wasted lightmap usage that could affect the bandwidth.

Typically, what happens is that smaller items that are easily overlooked accidentally get too much lightmap density. The lightmap density view mode have color indicators from blue for below optimal, to green for optimal, to red for too high. Brown-colored items are not considered in the calculation, as they are movable skeletal meshes. In Figure 8-17, we have increased the lightmap density on the selected object to the fourfold amount, to demonstrate how it shows up in red using the lightmap density view mode.

Figure 8-17. *Lightmap overshoot showing in red*

It should be noted that the commercial third-party plugin AutoLightmapUEr (www.unrealengine.com/marketplace/autolightmapuer) allows us to automatically calculate and assign lightmap properties to all scene objects according to its size in the world, thus making the process easier to handle on a large scene with high object counts.

The other two view modes—light complexity and light overlap—have less relevance for us, because we want to avoid anything but static lights. In the most extreme case, we would consider only one dynamic light maximum if absolutely necessary, so there would not ever be a chance for a complex lighting or light overlapping situation. Nevertheless, we can use these viewport modes to double check and verify that our scene is predominantly lit by static lights.

Starting the Profiling Stage

We continue with our strategy, having eliminated all possible areas of trouble during the early production stages, and move now into profiling our project's performance. We will start by doing that in the Unreal editor on our development PC. Even though we will later profile directly on the Android platform, it makes sense to occasionally profile the performance in the editor to detect possible performance spikes and to review the overall performance balance. If we are able to detect any problems here, it will for sure not get any better on the target Android platform.

The GPU Visualizer

The GPU visualizer is a great tool to break down the frame at any given time. Considering the fact that we are shooting for 60 fps, which equals 16.6 milliseconds per frame, the tools allows us to breakdown all GPU activity per frame in milliseconds. We can bring it up using Control-Shift-comma on the keyboard or by the profilegpu command using the console. Even though we are currently using it on the development PC and not the target platform, we can review the activity to spot excessive processing on specific tasks (see Figure 8-18).

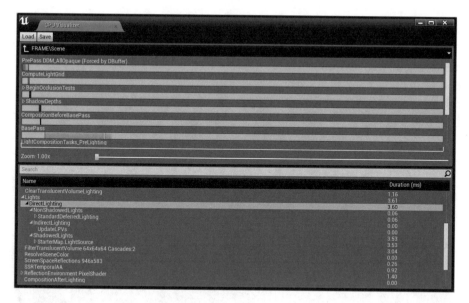

Figure 8-18.   *The GPU visualizer*

Typically, it would allow us to find lights that have accidently not been turned to static, or post-processing effects that would be active in the scene without being immediately obvious.

Using the Session Frontend

To get detailed information on the CPU activities, we will use the session front end that is available under the Developer Tools section in the Windows menu. Using the session front end, we can make stat captures of our project at runtime using *stat startfile* to start the capture and *stat stopfile* to end the capture from the console. Once we open the captured file, it allows us to review every possible CPU activity detail down to the individual Blueprint execution in milliseconds. Once again, we are looking for unusual spikes and excessive numbers to see if there is any item or event that could be optimized before reviewing it on the target platform, targeting 60 fps, or 16.6 milliseconds per frame (see Figure 8-19).

Figure 8-19. *Profiling using the session front end*

To get a performance overview in our viewport, we can use the console commands *stat fps* and *stat unit* to remove the stat display *stat none*. To get extended information on the game and rendering thread, we use the console commands *stat game* and *stat scenerendering*.

The Unreal documentation site has a complete list of all stat commands at `https://docs.unrealengine.com/en-us/Engine/Performance/StatCommands`.

Our goal is to identify items or events that may be a cause for performance bottlenecks and try to change, rearrange, or redesign the render elements or game logic, and get rid of the bottleneck.

Profiling on the Android Target Platform

Once everything possible is optimized on the development PC, we are ready to profile on the target platform. On mobile devices such as the Gear VR, it is easy to access the console by just removing the phone and using the four-finger tab gesture.

With the four-finger tab gesture, it is possible to access the console and type in any console command—just like on a desktop PC. Once the input command is completed, we can put the headset back on and continue. With a standalone headset, it gets a bit trickier as we don't have direct access to the screen, because it is not removable. The other problem is that we don't have any keyboard input. At the time of this writing, Bluetooth keyboards are not officially supported, but it is in some cases possible to hook up a keyboard using a sideloaded Android app that allows us to pair the keyboard in its settings.

Keyboard support for Oculus standalone headsets is expected in the near future; as such, we will not go into the specifics of the unofficial setup using the sideloaded apks. Even without using a keyboard, we can build controls into our project that allow us to access the most important profiling commands. Option number one is to temporarily insert an execute console command node *stat fps* in the Command field at event begin play followed by an execute console command *stat unit* node (see Figure 8-20).

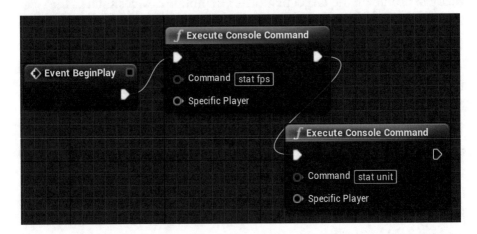

Figure 8-20. *Executing console commands from the level Blueprint*

An alternative, if we want more control over when to see the profiling stats, would be to hook it up to one of the Motion Controller buttons, if these are not all in use. For example, Thumbstick (R)Up (see Figure 8-21).

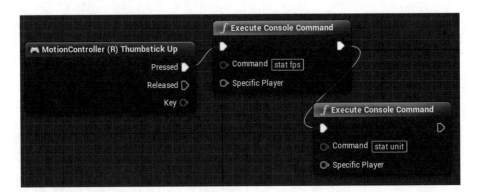

Figure 8-21. *Executing console commands with the motion controller*

If we want a number of different stat commands at our disposal, it would make sense to put together a custom menu using the UMG widget component, and either place it into the world or connect it to the VR pawn and activate it with a motion controller input action (see Figure 8-22).

Figure 8-22. *Creating a widget menu for console commands*

In the UMG Widget Graph editor, we set up the button events like any other events to trigger the execute console command nodes (see Figure 8-23).

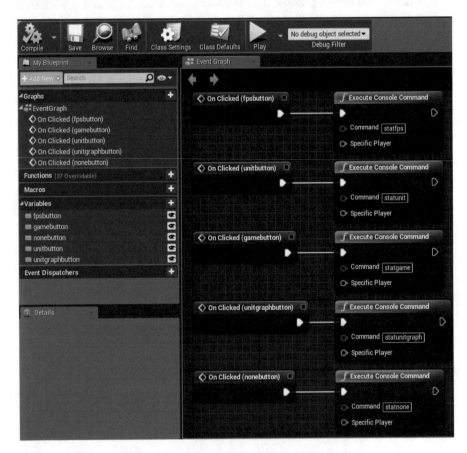

Figure 8-23. *Setting up the console command buttons*

Using the Oculus Metrics Tool

The Oculus Metrics tool is an Android app that gives a detailed report on the VR projects performance that are specific to the Oculus Android platform, including a number of values that we don't get from the Unreal profiling tools, such as temperature, indicating overheating and battery, to show drain.

On mobile VR headsets such as the Gear VR, it is easy to install it like any other apk file. Once installed, the app is launched as a regular Android app with two pages for settings and preferences. Once the Gear VR project is started, the settings will affect the currently running VR app. On standalone headsets such as the Oculus Go, we have to install the app using the adb command adb install -r -g OVRMetricsTool_v1.3.apk, which immediately gives us the stat overlay inside of the HMD. To toggle the overlay display on and off, use the adb command adb shell am start omms://settings, which launches the menu, to set visibility and preferences (see Figure 8-24).

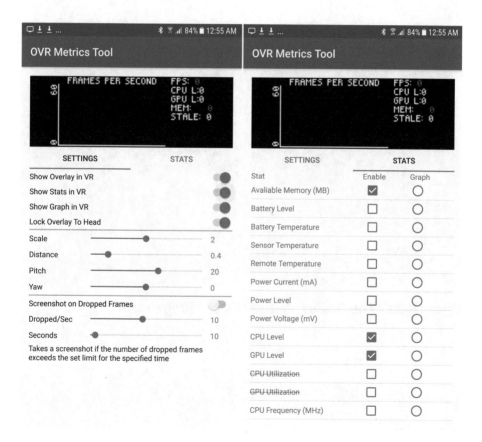

Figure 8-24. *Using the Oculus Metrics tool*

Similar to the Unreal session front end, we can start a profiling session, and depending on our profile settings, we are able to capture a detailed performance report (see Figure 8-25).

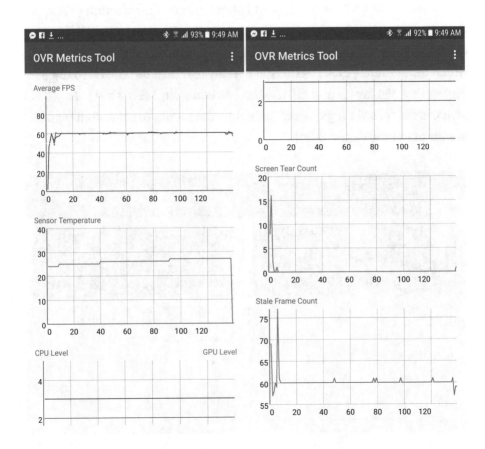

Figure 8-25. *The Oculus Metrics tool profiling charts*

Setting up the Oculus Monitor Application

The Oculus Monitor application is an additional tool that can be run from our PC using the adb connection over USB to initialize a capture session and subsequently load the captured file onto the PC app for review. The data is Oculus Android platform specific and includes temperature but also frame buffers, making it easier to visually identify the actual problem region when it occurs during gameplay. The chart overview makes it possible to identify and target bottlenecks (see Figure 8-26).

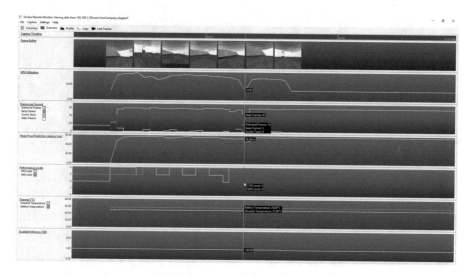

Figure 8-26. *Running the Oculus Monitor application*

Setting up RenderDoc to Analyze the Rendering Pipeline

After having identified the problem zone using the Unreal and Oculus profiling tools, we can zoom in to dissect the render pipeline using the third-party open source tool RenderDoc. Unless we were already able to sort out the performance issue by optimizing scene items and events, we can use this tool to dive deep into the individual render pipeline elements to investigate the cause of a performance problem. RenderDoc shows the complete render pipeline flowchart broken down into sections (see Figure 8-27).

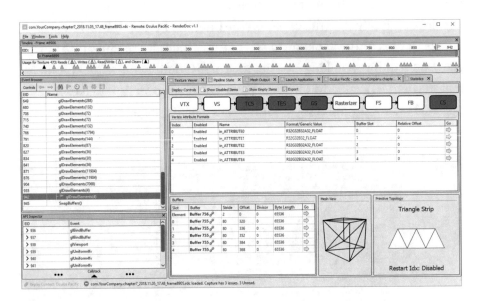

Figure 8-27. *Reviewing render pipeline elements with RenderDoc*

It is able to show individual draw calls for each stereoscopic frame. This makes it possible to review the render components that make up the final image and to decide if individual features or effects may actually be worth the cost by reviewing how efficiently the scene is built (see Figure 8-28).

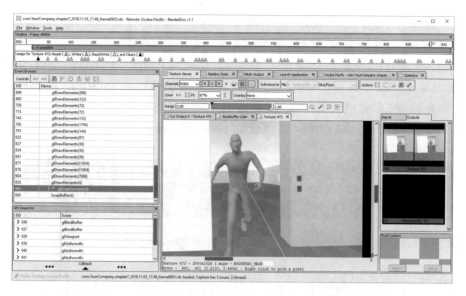

Figure 8-28. *Reviewing texture output in RenderDoc*

In addition, RenderDoc shows the mesh at different stages. We can explore input and output of the transform data, making possible its exploration as an interactive wireframe (see Figure 8-29).

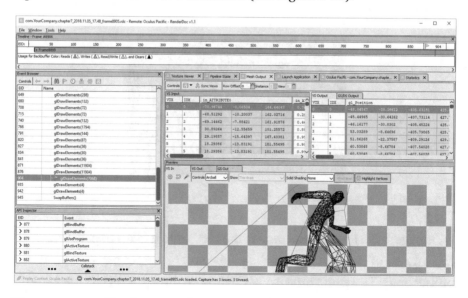

Figure 8-29. *Checking mesh output using RenderDoc*

Due to the deep insights that RenderDoc enables, it is also a good tool to use for exploring what kinds of graphic tricks other developers used on commercial titles to get the most performance mileage out of the platform. To use RenderDoc with Unreal, we enable it in the project settings under the Android Graphics Debug section in the Android tab and select RenderDoc from the drop-down menu (see Figure 8-30).

Figure 8-30. *Setting RenderDoc in the project settings*

Considerations and What to Watch Out For

Starting with the GPU and CPU profiler, we can identify early on if our project is GPU bound or CPU bound. If it is not clear whether the project is GPU bound or not, we start by having a look at the stat unit results (see Figure 8-31).

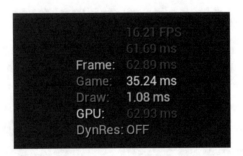

Figure 8-31. *Reviewing stat fps and stat unit*

In Figure 8-31, the frame time is the total time it takes to generate a single frame of the scene and is the equivalent of frames per second in milliseconds. The game time is the CPU game thread, which is the game logic, Blueprints, and so forth. The draw time shows the CPU render thread, which is the duration it takes the CPU to prepare the scene for rendering on the GPU. GPU shows the total time to process the frame on the GPU. The highest number is where the bottleneck is. The numbers are color coded as follows: green is OK, yellow is borderline, and red shows a problem.

In our example, the main bottleneck is the GPU, so we need to call up the GPU profiler to check which processes are taking the longest time. In this case, the problem was too many heavy post-processes. To fix the problem, we disable or delete them.

If the game number is too high, we should look at the CPU profiler and review our game logic. Common offenders are too many physics operations, too complex math, and/or too many large and complex Blueprints. Some nodes are sensitive to context. The Get All Actors Of Class node that we used in Chapter 6 worked great in the way we used it, but can slow down if there are large numbers of arrays in the scene. We should try to reduce spawning to on-load wherever possible, as it is expensive. We can look at what is ticking and evaluate if events triggers can be used instead of a constant tick. In some cases, if the Blueprints are too complex, they can be made native to run in C++ instead of the virtual machine (VM).

If the draw number is too high, it means the bottleneck is in the CPU render thread. To check scene complexity we can use the console command *stat initviews* to show the count of visible static mesh elements, and *stat rhi* to find out how many triangles are in the scene by looking at the *triangle drawn* line. We can analyze what is going on in the CPU render thread by using the session front end and reviewing the entries that are relevant to drawing. Most of the time, we have to reduce scene complexity or shader complexity. One way to test scene element is to use the Common Show Flags feature under the Show button in the viewport.

More show flags are listed in the documentation and can be called on the console (https://docs.unrealengine.com/en-us/Engine/UI/LevelEditor/Viewports/ShowFlags). By switching show/hide on the various viewport items and features, we can observe the reaction on the draw number and analyze the performance correlation accordingly. We should try to simplify geometry or to combine meshes or textures together and LOD levels.

We should consider removing items that the user cannot see, such as backsides. If we find the offender but don't know why exactly it is causing the bottleneck, we can to turn to RenderDoc to investigate deeper into the render pipeline and see what is going on in the individual draw calls and what must be changed to improve the performance.

Checklist

Let's put together a quick checklist for the case that we run into stubborn performance problems and are not sure if we have looked at all the possible solutions.

Let's check.

- Have meshes and materials been merged were possible?

- Have PBR textures been baked down to a color map where possible?

- Have modular instanced meshes been used for level design?

- Have LODs been generated for busy scenes and dense meshes?

- Are all lights set to static?

- Has the number of non-static lights been reduced to only the necessary ones?

- Are no post processes in the scene?

- Have texture sizes been optimized in the compression settings?

- Has automatic mip-mapping been accidentally turn-off or changed in the Texture editor?

- Have backsides and triangles not visible to user been removed?

- Has HDR been turned off in the Project Rendering section?

- Has transparent overdraw been reduced?

- Has unnecessary ticking been replaced by custom events?

- Has spawning been reduced to on-load?

- Is get *all actors of class* being used without large arrays?

- Have Blueprints been nativized in case of extensive Blueprints designs?

- Is multi-view and mobile multi-view enabled?

- Have distant environment meshes been baked to a skybox?

Waiting for Vulkan

The last point on the checklist should actually be this: *Has Vulkan support become available?* If so, then optimization becomes a whole different ballgame, with much more leeway regarding performance settings and draw call budgets. Vulkan is the much anticipated low-level graphics API successor to OpenGL. We can expect graphics that are more realistic, better battery duration, better consistency across platforms. Full Vulkan support for Oculus mobile and standalone VR using Unreal is expected to arrive soon.

Conclusion

In this chapter, we looked at the best ways to prepare our VR project to avoid problems. We looked at the typical issues that cause performance hits in mobile and standalone VR apps and identified areas, such as excessive foliage, particles, dynamic lights and shadows, to avoid. We looked at ways to make PBR textures more efficient by baking them into a color map, and we created custom blob shadows as a performance-friendly alternative to dynamic shadows.

We looked at how to optimize texture management and addressed the VR project settings that are performance relevant. We went through the most important profile tools provided by Unreal and Oculus and looked at the render pipeline using RenderDoc. Our goal was to develop a strategy when dealing with unexpected performance problems. In our strategy, we laid out a plan to first avoid problem areas to then profile on the development PC.

We then laid out how to tackle profiling on the target Android platform by setting up Blueprint events to execute console commands that let us access the profiling tools while running on the headset. Next, we used the Oculus toolset to profile specific issues including temperature and dropped frames. Using the Oculus monitor application, we were able to target the sensitive areas and close in on objects and events that caused performance drops.

Finally, we were able to analyze the problem areas by dissecting the graphics render pipeline by using RenderDoc which provided insights into individual draw calls. Using a set goal of 60 fps, we were able to analyze, target, and dissect problem areas, allowing us to identify events or object that caused problems, thus reaching our target performance. In an addendum we put together a list of important items to check, whenever we might run into performance trouble.

CHAPTER 9

Conclusion and Resources

Introduction

This last chapter of the book summarizes where we stand in the evolution of mobile and standalone VR and assesses what may be next. At this point, we can safely state that what we are witnessing is only the beginning of a new era of immersive media and that the rate of innovation will most likely accelerate rapidly once consumer adoption picks up.

One of the reasons for the expected acceleration is the synergy in related technology areas. We will look at the areas that are most likely to be important in the near-term future. After that, we will look at important resources for VR development, Oculus- and Unreal-specific online destinations, as well as VR news sites, CG resources, and asset libraries. Last but not least, we will look at some of the most important and influential books on these subjects.

Where Is Mobile and Standalone VR Headed?

Mobile and standalone VR is currently the choice for untethered, frictionless, consumer-friendly VR on the go. While VR development had a focus on high-end PC-based VR for a long time, the shift to mobile

© Cornel Hillmann 2019
C. Hillmann, *Unreal for Mobile and Standalone VR*,
https://doi.org/10.1007/978-1-4842-4360-2_9

Android-based systems is an important step toward a broader audience. The challenge is bringing the core magic of high-end VR to a mobile device with limited capabilities. This transition turns out to be a process of optimization and focus on the essential qualities of a VR experience. Let's not forget that this separation between tethered and mobile is only temporary. The endgame for all variations of VR is mobile anyway, whether through wireless transmission or enabled through the 5G cloud.

Mobile and Standalone VR Is Only Getting Started

Mobile and standalone VR development using Unreal is accelerating in efficiency and accessibility of the toolset. It is becoming increasingly feasible for small design studios or individual freelancers to build specialized VR applications to communicate ideas and utilize the potential of immersive storytelling. Interactive VR apps for marketing, education, and enterprise application have become possible to produce with smaller teams, on shorter timelines, without the typical coding bottleneck, thanks to the power and efficiency of the Blueprint system in Unreal. Building game logic with visual scripting is the part of the evolution that allows the next generation of immersive applications to be created by VR media designers.

Unreal and Unreal Studio are being adopted by design studios to extend their services from static visualization to fully interactive, real-time experiences. A technical artist who previously built solutions in Maya using MEL script will have no problem picking up Blueprints, and by doing that, expanding his toolset to bring his 3D creations to the next level.

VR is a great empowerment for 3D artists, as it allows the user to experience the scale of creations. As a 3D designer and world builder, you can live in your ideas, you are able to build your own reality. VR is accelerating the importance of CG art, as the immersive XR future will need a lot of assets to be built. As the interconnected XR world grows, it will need talent to innovate and ideas to reinvent designs and reimagine the visual language of interaction.

Let's not forget that we are today at the very first generation of standalone VR headsets. If we compare this perspective with the rapid evolution of the smartphone, from its humble first generation of devices, we can expect at least a similar revolution in technical breakthroughs and consumer adaptation.

The first generation of smartphones was clunky, hard to understand, slow, and tedious to operate. Today's standalone headsets already have a better head start, are much slicker and intuitive, and are being used in a lot of different ways by a growing fan base of enthusiasts. Nevertheless, for the average consumers to buy into it, quality needs to go up and friction has to come down. Consumers haven't really seen individual pixels on a screen in ages. Most consumers have become used to 4K TVs and high-definition mobile screens, and expect the same from any other devices, no matter what the technicalities are and what marvel it holds in other areas. But, similar to the first generation of smartphones, consumer VR still has to overcome difficult hurdles to get the attention and approval of consumers.

The emerging field of XR devices including VR, AR, and mixed-reality devices is on its way to finding consumer approval through experimentation and iteration, through throwing concepts against the wall until something sticks. As XR is taking shape, we still don't know its final form, which devices will dominate, or which application will be the most popular.

What Is Next?

It is sometimes overlooked that development and innovation in the XR ecosystem is not linear, but the result of synergy between complementary technologies that accelerate in dynamically connected developments.

Very often, disruptive technologies evolves behind closed doors and, once released to the market, trigger a rapid succession of innovation breakthroughs through its affiliation network effect. Let's look at some of the emerging trends that are not yet in the spotlight, but will have an enormous impact in the future once the larger XR environment is ready to support them.

The New Frontiers of Mixed-Reality XR

VR and AR are mostly addressing different areas in current developments, but that could change quickly. It was stated at a recent Magic Leap developer conference, that mixed realities between AR and VR have a lot of potential and benefits for consumers, especially in terms of e-sports applications. We already see the emergence of asynchronous gameplay apps such as *Covert*, where a VR player cooperates with a player using a tablet. It is safe to assume that we will see more mixed-reality environments, where users have the option to join using a VR headset on an AR device or any mobile device, such as a tablet or smartphone, sharing the same spatial playground (see Figure 9-1).

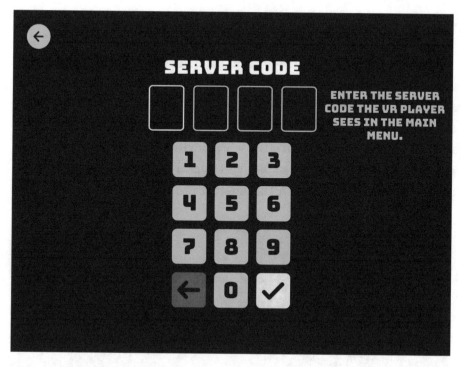

Figure 9-1. *Joining a VR headset with a tablet for co-op gameplay with Covert*

Developers using Unreal benefit once again from the high degree of SDK integration for the different platforms. Addressing the basic controller functions for the Magic Leap is not much different than for the Oculus Go. Mixed-reality environments, especially e-sport titles with a strong spatial factor, will open up opportunities for innovation that will draw more users.

The Coming WebVR Boom

The fact that WebVR apps are lightweight, and that no storefront doorkeepers can restrict access to them, makes the former ideal for experimentation, one-offs, and non-commercial showcases. As WebVR is mostly driven by open source software, its community has a distinct free, open-minded, and friendly spirit that helps motivate contributors.

Flexible, free, and easy-to-learn tools such as A-Frame (see Figure 9-2) allow users to build slick WebVR applications using HTML and JavaScript. A passionate and enthusiastic developer community is constantly pushing the boundaries of what is possible with WebVR. We can expect a diverse, rich, and highly connected WebVR world in the near future, where users can seamlessly travel between WebVR URLs to experience personal expressions, music videos, and original art show pieces.

Figure 9-2. *A WebVR experience build with A-Frame*

An additional showcase for a WebVR project using social mixed-reality is Hubs by the open source group Mozilla. It's a free, easy-to-use, multiplatform, VR chat room that allows users to log in from a VR web browser using a headset and be joined by any mobile device or PC. The open and accessible nature of the project is a prime showcase of what WebVR is capable of (see Figure 9-3).

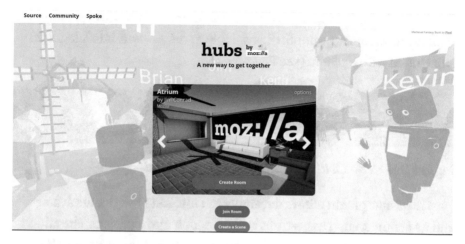

Figure 9-3. *Hubs by Mozilla*

Sharing a video with friends in a Hubs VR chat room is as easy as pasting a YouTube URL. The pasted URL gets automatically converted into a shared 3D scene object and can be moved and positioned anywhere in the chat room. It is currently the only app that lets users from any VR platform communicate with each other.

The Social Future of VR Is Centered Around the Avatar

Almost everyone in the XR industry agrees that the future of XR is social. For example, Facebook has defined the purpose of VR is to bring people together. Multiplayer VR titles are at the forefront of the social-VR vision. And, it has been shown that the social aspect of VR is important to users.

Central to the social experience is the avatar and how it conveys emotions. Oculus has made its avatar SDK, available to developers. It is integrated into Unreal with a plugin (see Figure 9-4).

Figure 9-4. *The Oculus avatar plugin in Unreal*

The avatar plugin allows developers to integrate the Oculus avatar and its features, such as gestures and lip-synch into a project. The added benefit for users is a consistent experience with their avatar across VR applications. Oculus is constantly improving its avatar feature set and we can expect them to be at the forefront of the next wave of consumer avatars (see Figure 9-5).

Figure 9-5. *The Oculus avatar customizer*

Avatars are destined to become a consumer phenomenon, most likely only comparable to the smartphone selfie explosion. Avatars are a form of self expression and a way for users to present themselves in an idealized way. Avatar technology will become highly accelerated once eye tracking and user photo-mapping becomes available.

Productivity and the Virtual Workspace

It may turn out that productivity applications are the killer apps that the industry is waiting for. Virtual reality as a tool to increase productivity is clearly on the rise with virtual desktop apps, virtual meetings, and screen sharing, as shown by the Bigscreen app (see Figure 9-6).

Figure 9-6. *Meeting in Bigscreen*

VR meetings make a good alternative to group calls by adding presence and gestures to an online discussion. Virtual desktop and office applications allow the user to focus in a busy environment and may be the future of the cubicle. Even a simple reading app—such as virtual book reader (see Figure 9-7)—can add surprising value in the right situation, as it lets the reader navigate in new ways while reading.

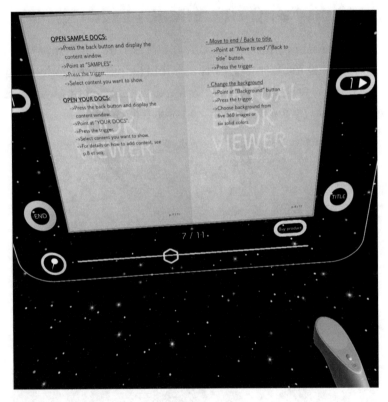

Figure 9-7. *The virtual book reader*

These solutions are the forerunner of a future workspace that lets the user customize his workplace, media, and socials environment in VR. The design industry is already using VR in the production process for modeling, asset creation, and level creation. Allegorithmic recently showcased a hybrid demo version of Substance Painter that is part VR 3D view and part 2D workspace. We will most likely see more concepts like that, combining the best of both worlds.

VR Enhanced by Artificial Intelligence

The artificial intelligence revolution has made its way into many unexpected areas of digital content creation, from image processing to the de-noising of high-end renderings. An emerging new area is AI-driven VR host for B2B service applications. The Amazon Web Services (AWS) cloud platform opened its VR creation tool, called Sumerian, in 2017. It allows you to publish platform agnostic WebVR and AR applications using a visual state machine to create dynamic interactions. Sumerian integrates with other AWS tools, including some of AWS's artificial intelligence tools. Notable examples are the deep-learning tools for speech recognition and facial analysis to build complex interactions with the user (see Figure 9-8).

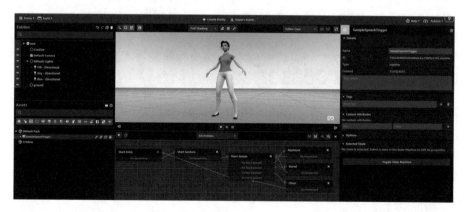

Figure 9-8. *Designing VR interaction in Amazon AWS Sumerian's AI tools*

The system is intended to be used for virtual help desks or point-of-sale assistance in VR and AR applications.

Live Volumetric Video Holograms

Volumetric video is one the new exciting frontiers of AR and VR. Making it possible to capture a person as a moving volumetric 3D object and transmitting that captured performance is a challenging task on the bleeding edge of what is possible with today's technology. In a way, volumetric video holograms are moving photogrammetry objects. A point cloud is captured, polygon geometry is created, and captured textures are projected on the geometry, 30 to 60 times a second. Considering the process it takes to create just one quality photogrammetry object makes this sound like a daunting endeavor to enable the process for moving objects on a high frame-rate.

The much discussed New Zealand startup 8i has pioneered this technology, but it will most likely take a few more iterations to become consumer friendly enough to be adopted by the broader market. Nevertheless, the promise is intriguing, as this approach to social VR could bring a new angle to VR meetings and the virtual office concept.

Haptic VR Accessories

Haptic VR accessories have found their place in high-end VR. They are mostly used in VR arcades. VR treadmills such as the Virtuix Omni give a high-end VR experience the extra edge in immersion by solving the VR locomotion problem in an intuitive way. HTC Vive pioneered the VR accessories field by introducing the Vive tracker in 2017. It allowed developers to build additional accessories tracked by the Vive's lighthouse system.

At some point, we can expect the broader consumer market to adopt similar add-on systems that allow you to expand the home experience with additional tracked objects. This could open up an accessory market, similar to the success story of the Nintendo Wii with its expandable controller add-on ecosystem. First steps will most likely be variations of the controllers with different form factors, as we have seen with the Sony PSVR and the popular AIM controller (see Figure 9-9).

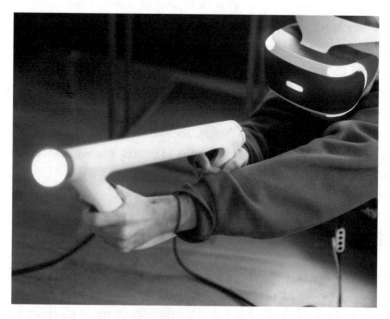

Figure 9-9. *Sony PSVR's AIM controller (photo by C. Hillmann)*

As the exact form of the controller is mirrored in the VR world, it adds an extra layer of immersive presence to the experience through the haptic feedback of the device.

5G and the VR Cloud

5G networks are coming and will enable super-fast streaming with low latency. The initial latency is expected to be 20 milliseconds, which is good enough for casual interaction. Once 5G pixel streaming with low latency reaches mobile and standalone headsets, the heavy lifting of high-end graphics processing can be done in the cloud, while the headset is used as an interactive playback device. This will break mobile headsets free from the limitations of underpowered mobile chipsets. Extreme high-end graphics, with massive scene geometry and shader complexity, will bring mobile headsets to a completely new level and enable large and graphics-heavy multiplayer online worlds, such as Sansar, the Second Life successor.

Unreal version 4.21 introduced pixel streaming, which allows users to run an application in the cloud and stream it to browser clients for high-quality interactivity. While it is not yet available for VR applications, it is for sure the next logical step to integrate this technology with VR apps. Applications (such as Riftcat, VRidge, and Virtual Desktop) that stream from a desktop to a VR headset using Wi-Fi are the forerunners of this development.

Unreal as a Full DCC Production Suite

Unreal plays a key role in the transition of the DCC industry from render farm–based pipelines to real-time production. The added muscle in post-production and DCC tools is helping VR development in indirect ways. For example, scenes built for a VR project can be used for high-end cinematics and trailer footage. General-purpose, third-party rigging tools such as the Allright Rig (see Figure 9-10) that allow users to do all the rigging and character animation within the Unreal environment are just as useful for a VR production as they are for any other gaming project.

Figure 9-10. *Unreal as a character animation suite with a third-party plugin*

The extended toolset for virtual studio production and postproduction allow VR content creators to leverage their skillsets in a highly integrated production environment that offers more ways to repurpose content and integrate production techniques. For example, the public Tello roadmap for Unreal reveals that subdivision modeling tools are planned for the engine to enable polygon editing without having to leave the Unreal environment.

Resources

Let's look at the most useful resources when it comes to VR production and learning, and the broader context of XR ideas and visions.

Unreal Resources

Unreal Get Started with UE4 (`https://docs.unrealengine.com/en-US/ GettingStarted`) is online documentation that covers every aspect of Unreal development, including Android and VR.

Unreal Engine Online Training (`https://academy.unrealengine.com`) is a resource that includes Unreal learning videos and an in-depth tutorial series on the most important areas of game production.

Oculus Resources

The following are Oculus resources.

- The Oculus Unreal Getting Started Guide (`https:// developer.oculus.com/documentation/unreal/ latest/concepts/unreal-getting-started-guide/`). Oculus has recently updated the guide for Unreal with numerous get-started and help files. The covered items are basic, but provide some fundamental setup routines. Hopefully, this resource will be expanded in the future.

- The Oculus Developer Blog (`https://developer. oculus.com/blog`). The Oculus blog offers a lot of interesting insights on recent software updates and developer perspectives. Detailed project post-mortems reveal how developers of recent commercial releases tackled some of the challenges in mobile VR.

- The Oculus YouTube channel (`www.youtube.com/ user/oculusvr`). The Oculus YouTube channel features not only teasers, trailers, and playthroughs, but also developer insights and talks from recent Oculus Connect conferences.

VR News and Reviews

The following are virtual reality news resources.

- UploadVR (`https://uploadvr.com`). A consumer-oriented VR news site. Covers all platforms, including mobile and standalone VR with reviews and product news.

- Road to VR (`www.roadtovr.com`). Similar to UploadVR, covers the latest VR news for trends, products and upcoming titles.

- VRScout (`https://vrscout.com`). Covers industry news and reviews.

- VRFocus (`www.vrfocus.com`). Covers reviews and product updates.

VR Podcasts

The following are VR podcasts.

Voices of VR Podcast (`voicesofvr.com`) is a highly recommended quality podcast channel with in-depth talks covering not only developer perspectives, but also cultural, futuristic areas where VR has an impact.

The podcast by the VR/AR Association (`www.thevrara.com/podcast`) has interesting insights from industry guests from all areas of the VR and AR ecosystem.

Third-Party Unreal YouTube channels

Mathew Wadstein Tutorials (`www.youtube.com/channel/UCOVfF7PfLbRdV EmOhONTrNQ`) is a great resource for people new to Unreal. Mathew Wadstein covers a lot of essential Unreal features in short informative video clips.

Mitch's VR Lab (`www.youtube.com/channel/UChvlNUgZKmEd-Gul_Tdv8Uw`) is by Mitchell McCaffrey, the author of the *Unreal Engine VR Cookbook*. On his YouTube channel, he explores a lot of the typical VR setup and interaction topics.

Reddit VR Discussions

The following leads to relevant discussions on Reddit.

- `Reddit.com/r/virtualreality`
- `Reddit.com/r/oculus`
- `Reddit.com/r/GearVR`
- `Reddit.com/r/OculusGo`
- `Reddit.com/r/OculusQuest`

The Oculus- and VR-related Reddit channels are very active and provide a lot of user feedback, tips, tricks, and information that can't be found anywhere else.

VR Developer Forums

The VR development section in the Unreal online forum (`https://forums.unrealengine.com/development-discussion/vr-ar-development`) is an essential resource to stay on top of recent updates, bug fixes, tips, tricks and workarounds.

The Oculus developer forum (`https://forums.oculusvr.com/developer/`) is an important resource to track updates and issues with the Oculus SDK and to get developer insights.

CG Production Resources

CGSociety (https://cgsociety.org) is an industry portal to all things CG, including news, tutorials, VFX breakdowns, artist spotlights, and forums.

ArtStation (www.artstation.com) is the leading showcase platform for CG artists.

The Polycount Newsfeed (https://polycount.com) features 3D game art community with news, interviews, and forums.

The Blender Artists Community (https://blenderartists.org) is large Blender artist forum with sections on Python, jobs, add-on support, and tutorials.

Online Resources for 3D Assets

Previously run by Google, now operated by Trimble Inc., 3D Warehouse (https://3dwarehouse.sketchup.com) is a free online model resource. Models can not only be downloaded in the sketchup format but also in the Collada, interchange format that Blender supports. Model quality varies from the very basic to the occasional gem that can be used as a starting point for building a scene.

The following are other 3D assets resources.

- Free3D (https://free3d.com). Free downloads in a variety of formats.

- Archive3D (https://archive3d.net). Free models in 3DS format.

- cgtrader (https://cgtrader.com). Commercial premium models.

- GrabCAD (https://grabcad.com). CAD-oriented site with a large download section.

- Sketchfab (https://sketchfab.com/store). The store section of the 3D online community.

- TurboSquid (www.turbosquid.com). One of the longest-running commercial 3D model sites.

Essential Books

Mitch McCaffrey's *Unreal Engine VR Cookbook* (Addison-Wesley Professional, 2017) is packed with in-depth technical information on VR development with Unreal. Even though his book is focused on PC-based VR, a lot of information applies to mobile and standalone, as well.

The VR Book: Human-Centered Design for Virtual Reality by Jason Jerald (Morgan & Claypool Publishers-ACM, 2015) gives a great overview over the broad spectrum of VR from history, to experimental areas and UX considerations. It is one of the most complete works on the subject from a nontechnical perspective. It focuses on the rules and principles that are important in the process of understanding and designing VR experiences.

The Fourth Transformation: How Augmented Reality and Artificial Intelligence Change Everything by Robert Scoble and Shel Israel (CreateSpace Independent Publishing Platform, 2016) is a highly speculative book on the near-term implications of emerging technologies in mixed realities and AI. It is primarily aimed at business decision makers who are not familiar with broader technology trends, and it explains how disruptive change will transform the digital landscape.

Experience on Demand: What Virtual Reality Is, How It Works, and What It Can Do by Jeremy Bailenson (W. W. Norton & Co., 2018) gives a good overview over the wider scope of VR, where it is coming from, and where it is headed. It gives a good understanding of the big picture and addresses a lot of fundamental questions concerning the real-life implication of VR.

Future Presence: How Virtual Reality Is Changing Human Connection, Intimacy, and the Limits of Ordinary Life by *Wired* editor Peter Rubin (HarperOne, 2018) offers a macro view on the implications of VR. It is a good introduction and primer on the subject for people interested in a wider perspective of VR.

Dawn of the New Everything: Encounters with Reality and Virtual Reality by Jaron Lanier (Henry Holt and Co., 2017) is a very personal memoir by one of the most influential thinkers and brightest minds of our era. Lanier writes about his early days as pioneer of VR. As one of the co-founders of the early but short-lived VR company VLP Research, his prototypes were featured in the 1992 VR sci-fi action horror film classic *The Lawnmower Man.*

Masters of Doom: How Two Guys Created an Empire and Transformed Pop Culture by David Kushner (Random House, 2003) is about the fascinating history of game technology legends John D. Carmack and John Romero. Carmack, CTO of Oculus and a major driving force behind VR and especially mobile and standalone VR, had a dramatic impact on the 3D game engine revolution when *Wolfenstein 3D* and *Doom* were released, based on his technological breakthroughs. The book explores the ups and downs of the relationships and obstacles the early partnership was facing and what led to the innovations that finally transformed pop culture.

Game Engine Black Book: Wolfenstein 3D by Fabien Sanglard (CreateSpace Independent Publishing, 2018) is sort of a technological archeology research adventure, unearthing the early days of the breakthroughs of John Carmack's Wolfenstein game engines.

Ready Player One by Ernest Cline (Crown, 2011) is probably the most influential young adult work of contemporary VR fiction and the base for the successful Steven Spielberg movie of the same name. The Oasis, the VR online world described in the book, is one of the very-often quoted VR references.

Snow Crash by Neal Stephenson (Del Rey, 2000) is a VR sci-fi classic originally published in 1992 and often referenced when talking about VR. The often-used term *Metaverse* was coined by Stephenson in this novel.

Numerous tech startups and VR projects reference terms from the classic novel. For example, the Amazon AWS VR/AR engine is rumored to have taken its name *Sumerian* from a *Snow Crash* reference.

Neuromancer by William Gibson (Ace, 1984) is probably the best-known classic sci-fi novel with a VR, matrix, and cyberpunk theme and a huge influence on pop culture and techno-dystopian aesthetics.

Conclusion

In this final chapter, we discussed where the industry is headed, we gave an outlook on the emerging trends, and which dynamic subsections in immersive XR will most likely affect the development and evolution of mobile and standalone VR.

In the resources section, we listed the most important online channels for accessing learning materials from Unreal, Oculus, and third parties, and looked at related areas, such as CG and online asset libraries. With a list of recommended books, not only technical, but also looking at the broader context, as well as including often-quoted classic VR sci-fi literature, we concluded our resource listings and this book.

Exciting times are ahead of us, and as developers and creators, we are lucky to have powerful and free-to-use tools as the Unreal Engine and the DCC software such as Blender at our disposal. The tools have matured over decades and the content creation ecosystem has become user friendly enough to empower a new generation of creators. As technology innovation is accelerating, human imagination gets inspired and gives rise to endlessly evolving new concepts and ideas. Never before have humans had the ability to completely create their own reality—a reality that can be lived in and experienced. Be prepared to be amazed and to amaze others.

We are in for a wild ride into the unknown. This is a great time to understand and learn the tools used to convert imagination into experiences.

Index

P, Q

R

Printed in the United States
By Bookmasters